Breathe and Speak

A Scene Book for Actors

Breathe and Speak

A Scene Book for Actors

Marc Clopton

Dedication

This book is dedicated to all the actors in my studio who have for over twenty years inspired me to write. You have taught me more about humanity than I thought I had the right to know.

Special Thanks

This book would never be if not for my friend Gene Bua, who gave me permission to say "I don't know." Thank you, Gene, for giving me a forum in which to test myself as an actor and as a writer.

Acknowledgements

To Ron Pullins for suggesting I do this book. And for giving me a deadline.

To Leslie Powell for being excited that I said, "Yes."

To Leslie Beauregard, whose organizational skills, computer savvy and awesome "can do" attitude made the actual writing of the book a joy.

In the mind of the beginner there are many possibilities, in the expert's there are few.

—Shunryu Suzuki Roshi

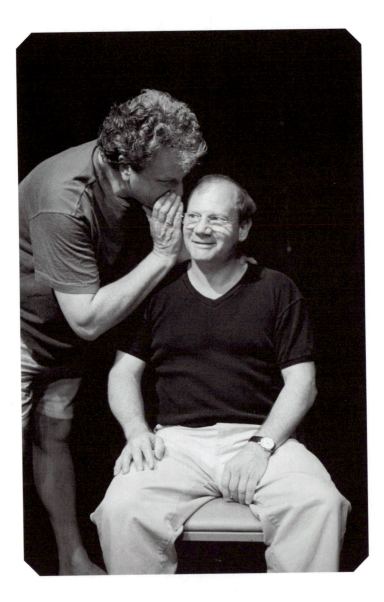

Contents

Note from the Author

In the following scenes, these characters can be male or female:

    The Rug – Bobbie

    Goodbye MacDougal – One

    Working Late – Entity

Preface

In the many places I have taught acting, one truth has remained constant. Whatever I think I might know about another person is laughable. Also, how and when and why a certain script ends up in the hands of a certain actor is a marvelous mystery. Even in my own classes when I'm picking the material.

When that script finds that actor, I see something I've never seen before; something I couldn't have anticipated; something that takes my breath away. As a result, over the years, I have become freer and freer with the script choices I make for my students. I give each student every kind of character to play, every type of scene and situation. And we've had every sort of result, from calamity to transcendence, and learned to absorb them all.

In his book, *The Shifting Point*, Peter Brook says, "I have never believed in a single truth. Neither my own, nor those of others… But I have discovered that one can only live by a passionate, and absolute identification with a point of view".

My unshakable belief is this: Every human being possesses the capacity to be fully, emotionally expressed. Also, no single actor comes to the table with more or better humanity than any other. Some find it easier to express than others.

How do you get it flowing? How do you get it to come out? How do you teach someone to trust their own feelings and to follow their own impulses? You get them up there on stage. Get them connecting with the text, finding out what it feels like and give them many different experiences with a good variety of material.

I offer this book of scenes as a compliment to the rich library of American plays from which we draw our inspiration.

These scenes are not associated with any well-known performances or high profile productions. There is no one to mimic. There is no award winning performance to erase from the mind's eye. There is no scholarly interpretation to fall back on. Given that, they add an interesting dimension to the work. I hope you enjoy them and find them useful.

Introduction

Much of my work in theater has been in training actors. The scenes and monologues in this book have, for the most part, grown out of my acting workshops. As with learning many academic subjects, craft skills, and sports, every actor learns *how to* differently. These scenes are not intended to be experienced in a vacuum. They are a complementary part of the vast arsenal of dramatic literature available to us today. In the short run, some academicians may disagree with me on the primacy of the actor. In the long run, I think we may find that we are not so far apart.

Some actors are drawn into the moment by their appreciation for and understanding of the literary context of the play. On the other end of the spectrum, some actors learn best by throwing themselves into a scene and finding out about it through encounters with the other actors and by encountering their own emotions and intuition. Between those two extremes, we can agree, there are countless variations. The point is, if you're an actor, you want to give yourself every opportunity to succeed.

The short story writer Grace Paley says of writing: "We write what we don't know we know". The novelist Italo Calvino speaks of a voice that comes from "somewhere beyond the book, beyond the author…from the unsaid, from what the world has not yet said of itself and does not yet have the words to say." The same can be said of actors and acting. We plumb the depths of our selves to find what we don't yet know and to discover what we have not been capable of until the very moment it happens. If we can say, "I don't know", without shame or apology then we can open ourselves to create a capacity, a skill, a presence of our own that might not have been.

I believe that one advantage of working with open scenes is that there is no specific target in mind. You have to rely on your own sense of what feels authentic, both in yourself and in your scene partner. By practicing this, in addition to your regular scene study, you will build confidence in knowing what is unique to you. I believe this confidence promotes a willingness to go beyond what you already know you can do.

To maximize the workout, the scenes contain little to no stage directions or indications regarding specific emotions. You will be saying, "I don't know" to many details of the scene. This is on purpose. You must trust both the text and yourself, your partner, and the moment.

There is a method to the madness of exercising this way. You become intimate with your own instrument and learn to be guided by internal sensations without anticipating a specific outcome. This does not make for sloppy and inconsistent acting, as you might fear. Quite the contrary. This process allows you to be very specific in performance without losing the quality of the first time experience.

Developing internal awareness and flexibility, you will not only be more available to the specifics of your character when you do perform a full-length play, you will also be more directable. This may seem like a statement of the obvious. I believe that the better you know your own instrument, the more accessible you are to different directors, no matter what their background, training or style might be.

I hope that you find, as my students have found, that you are so much more than you could know at this moment.

Giving Yourself the Premise

The premise is the bare bones *who, what, where* of the scene. Do not embellish the premise with judgments about the characters or choose one major emotion. We rarely feel just one emotion at a time. Just make sure that the information of the premise is connected with the feeling in your belly – whatever the feeling is.

You want the premise to be from the subjective point of view of your character, i.e.:

> *I am a man, she is a woman; we have a relationship, she is my wife. We are in the bedroom.*

Or…

> *I am a woman, he is a man; we have a relationship, I don't know what it is. We are in a train station.*

What you don't say to yourself is something like this:

> *I am a female cop and he's my asshole boss. We're at work. This is both external "female cop", and judgmentally limiting "asshole boss", and not specific "we're at work".*

The effective way to premise this scene would be:

> *I am a woman, he is a man; we have a relationship, we are both police officers, he is my boss. We are in his office.*

It may be very obvious in the script that the boss character is a jerk, but if you put that in the premise, it becomes a conclusion made before the action of the scene takes place. This is where the actor must trust that the additional information is in the text and will be revealed. Otherwise, you're at risk of playing only one note of the scene and keeping the characters two-dimensional.

Premising the use of drugs and alcohol

If it is stated that your character is under the influence of drugs or alcohol, be specific about it. This is an adjustment to the premise, so it comes after the who, what, where. If it's alcohol, choose an amount and type, i.e.: Three shots of bourbon, two glasses of wine, or three beers. If it is marijuana: *"I've had a J"*, or

" *a couple of tokes*". If it is acid, uppers, downers, ecstasy, heroin or cocaine, be specific. Breathe and give your body permission to respond. Trust your body. It will register an effect. Avoid playing the condition and let it happen.

The Fantastic Premise

A fantastic premise is when you are playing something like an alien, a ghost, God, an angel, or if you are in a fantastic setting like a parallel dimension or in heaven or in hell. You want the premise to initiate in you a specific feeling and/or point of view. You don't need to know exactly what that feeling is going to be like – stay open to experience the unexpected.

Bella, in the piece "Kingdom Come," can be seen as a guardian angel or a spirit guide. She's quirky, but she has a specific purpose in the scene. So even though she's not easily defined, make a choice that you can feel as personal.

> *I am a woman spirit, he is a man; we have a relationship, I am his spirit guide. We are meeting for the first time. We are at an inter-dimensional doorway.*

"I am his spirit guide" connects Bella to Steve.

In the piece "Russia in G", the spirit of Tchaikowski visits Gregor, a poet in Communist Russia. Is he there out of compassion for a man he identifies with or is he there to complete something so his spirit can move on?

The adjustment you can give yourself can give the encounter a specific purpose.

> Tchaikowski's premise is: *I am Peter Illiaich Tchaikowski, he is a man; we are meeting for the first time. We are in his apartment.*

Possible adjustments to the premise could be:

> *I must keep him from giving up.*

Or…

> *I can help him see past his own bleak perceptions.*

Keep it simple and make it personal.

Male/Female
Scenes

amy roemer '01

A Fine Line

Premise: **He** I am a man, she is a woman; we have a relationship, she is my lover. We are in our apartment.

She I am a woman, he is a man; we have a relationship, he is my lover. We are in our apartment. My opening is a success.

Hillary:	God! It went so well, Jack. Nobody expected it.
Jack:	What did they expect?
Hillary:	You know what I mean. What the hell's the matter with you?
Jack:	Nothing. I'm happy for you. It just seems... You shouldn't be surprised...
Hillary:	I'm pleased Jack. That's all. It's gratifying. You know what it's like. I wish you'd stayed longer. Maxine and George came in. They asked about you.
Jack:	That's nice. I'll call him. I'll see you later.
Hillary:	Where are you going?
Jack:	Racquetball.
Hillary:	We're expected at Cielle's for dinner. Frederick and Rosilyn are going to be there. They want to take my work to their gallery in Washington.
Jack:	I can't go to every event. I've got my own life to consider. Gotta stay in shape.
Hillary:	You're full of shit.
Jack:	Oh really? I'm late.
Hillary:	Talk to me. Don't go play racquetball. What's the matter.
Jack:	Nothing is the matter. We're the Renaissance couple. Two orbs circling the same apartment. No old fashioned attachments, no limitations, no expectations.

Hillary:	Of course we've had expectations…for good reason. Jack, I'm sorry things aren't working out the way you want yet. But you've got to keep trying…don't give up on yourself.
Jack:	Don't give me a speech. Your success is too new, your wisdom hasn't got enough miles on it yet.
Hillary:	You're jealous. Wow, I didn't expect this. People like my work so they're buying it. You keep writing music, keep creating. If you want a market, you'll find a market, but you have to keep creating. I wish you weren't jealous. I wish you could throw your arms around me and say, "I'm happy for you, Hillary". That's what I'd like, but that's not going to happen, is it?
Jack:	I knew this would happen. I could have written the script.
Hillary:	Go on – go play racquetball, Jack.
Jack:	Don't act so hurt. You got what you wanted.
Hillary:	You better pack some clothes.
Jack:	What?
Hillary:	You heard me. Don't come back.
Jack:	I'm gonna go play racquetball. We'll talk later, if you get home before two.
Hillary:	No, we'll talk now or we don't talk.
Jack:	Don't start laying down fucking ultimatums.
Hillary:	I didn't start with an ultimatum, I just want to talk to you. You want to play fucking racquetball.
Jack:	You're going to dinner.
Hillary:	Not 'til 7:00.
Jack:	I don't know Hill – I don't know if I can handle this.
Hillary:	What, me being a success?
Jack:	That combined with me being an as-yet-undiscovered-talent. Isn't that what your agent called me?
Hillary:	We can get through this, Jack.
Jack:	Can we? Can I? You're doing great – it's me. When the chips are down, I'm a fuckin' creep. I hate myself.
Hillary:	It's okay, I understand.
Jack:	Will you please not say that. It's not okay. You just told me to leave.
Hillary:	You're right. It's not okay, but I believe it could be okay again. Do you love me?
Jack:	Loving you isn't enough.
Hillary:	It is for me. Do you love me?

Jack:	I don't feel like I know you anymore. And I wonder if I was more in love with our struggle as artists, your nobility. I don't know why I feel so different now.
Hillary:	Should I take that as a "no"?
Jack:	I love you. I do.
Hillary:	Then this is worth talking about. I love you – very much.
Jack:	Before this, on my bad days I could look at you and think, "she's staying with it. If she can tough it out, so can I". Now on my bad days you're not there struggling beside me, and I feel alone. One little doubt creeps in and I start to unravel inside – you start to look like the enemy to me. Like you've forgotten the struggle already, and if the struggle is so easy to forget, why am I so invested in it? I'm doubting myself. I go so deep down into this emptiness that I look like a stranger to myself. It terrifies me.
Hillary:	I want this to be our life, not my life running parallel to your life.
Jack:	We haven't really thought of it that way.
Hillary:	Can we? Do you want that?
Jack:	I want to feel together again. Like we're both living in the same life. Together.

Another Night

Premise: **He** I am a man, she is a woman; we have a
relationship, we used to be lovers. We are in my
apartment.

She I am a woman, he is a man; we used to be
lovers. We are in his apartment. My boyfriend just
left me. I have been using cocaine and speed and have
been drinking whiskey.

Janice: Frank, Frankie my pal. Palsie Wowsie Frankie Spankie.

Frank: Janice. How'd you get in here? What happened?

Janice: Happened. What happened he asked.

Frank: Never mind, don't want to know.

Janice: Nothing. Nothing happened. Nothing of any significance ever
happened in her whole entire life. Must you remind me?

Frank: Straighten up, will you. What did you do?

Janice: What d'ya mean what did I do. I didn't do anything.

Frank: What are you on?

Janice: Oh. Nothin' much. A few drinks.

Frank: For three days?

Janice: A little coke.

Frank: What else?

Janice: Why does there have to be anything else?

Frank: You can't afford three days of coke.

Janice: A couple uppers. No biggie.

Frank: Jesus – you trying to kill yourself?

Janice: I was waiting for you. Where you been?

Frank: Touring. You know that.

Janice: Yeah.

Frank:	Why are you here, Jan?
Janice:	He's gone, Frank. Gone. Gone. Gone. My rock. My man. My loverboy. He crept right inside my soul and exposed every nerve. Made me feel. Made me think there might be a bright side to all of this. Then he split. I've been up for three days waiting for you to get home.
Frank:	I'll take you home. You can sleep it off.
Janice:	No, no, no, no. Don't take me home. I don't want to be alone. I can't face another night alone, Frankie. Please, not another night without him, without you.
Frank:	You're confused.
Janice:	Yes I am. Very terribly confused. Can you help me, Frank? Help me straighten out this terrible confusion. What is this bullshit crap about love, who made up this lie, Frankie? What fucked up little fruitcake started this lie about love bein' a good thing?
Frank:	Come on, I'll take you home. We're not solving any riddles tonight. I'm tired and you're drunk.
Janice:	No.
Frank:	Janice, I've been on the road two weeks, a show every night. I can't stand here and fight with you, come on.
Janice:	No, not another night.
Frank:	It's not just tonight. You fall for scumbags, Jan, charming spineless scum who can only get it up if they're high. You weren't in love. You couldn't have been in love; you never saw each other straight. You were always high.
Janice:	That's not true.
Frank:	Don't cry to me about losing the love of your life, it's not heartache you're feeling, it's withdrawal. Your loverboy, all your loverboys just take you away from it all. Get you stoned and then fuck their fantasies, it's not even you they're in bed with.
Janice:	You fucking faggot creep! Who the hell do you think you are? You're no stinking saint.
Frank:	Look, you're baked. I'm not gonna take that personally.
Janice:	You learn that in the program, you asshole?
Frank:	Yes, as a matter of fact. I've done the drugs, the booze and fucked just about anything that walked. So don't act like I don't know what I'm talkin' about.
Janice:	You don't know shit about me.
Frank:	I was you. I was a drunk junkie whore just like you.
Janice:	You punk. You fuckin' piece o' shit.

Frank: I'm the only one in your sorry life tellin' you the truth. What you're doing isn't working.

Janice: It's not fair Frankie. This cocksucking world just ain't a fair place.

Frank: No, it's not always, but what are you doing about it? You're the only one who can change how you feel.

Janice: I don't know where to start.

Frank: If you can stay sober 'til my next gig, you can start singing with me. Get focused again.

Janice: I'm not very nice. I'm sorry. You're good, Frank. You're good. But you know that, don't you? Good people know they're good.

Frank: I wouldn't know.

Janice: Yes you do. You have confidence, never have a bad night's sleep. I'm not jealous or anything.

Frank: You knew me when I was usin'.

Janice: Yeah, but you always had that thing. I'm just wondering what it must be like to be you.

Frank: It's not so great bein' me. I'm not so good. That's not what I'm sayin'. If I know anything of value at all, I learned it by fuckin' up. I'm not better than you, or anybody. I just got tired of fuckin' up.

Janice: I'm tired too. I want my life back.

Frank: It's yours for the takin'.

Barrie's Song

Premise: **He** I am a man, my name is Jack; I'm on the roof of my apartment building. I'm thinking about jumping.

                    She I am a woman, he is a man; we have a relationship, we were lovers when I died. We are on the roof of his apartment building.

Barrie:	Jackie boy?
Jack:	Barrie? Is this real?
Barrie:	Have I ever been anything but real? Come here Jackson; let me get a little taste of you. Lover boy. Love me Jackie. There's only me and you. Give me what you got, son, I want it all.
Jack:	You got it all. God, don't light a spark in me now.
Barrie:	God has nothin' to do with it.
Jack:	I wish I knew.
Barrie:	Don't go getting deep on me. This world is too fucked up.
Jack:	Is that why?
Barrie:	Why what?
Jack:	You died?
Barrie:	Hey, I'm here with you now. Don't get off the track.
Jack:	What's happening? Why are you here? I loved you. You could have tried.

(Flashback begins)

Barrie:	I'm just one person. Together we're just two people. We're talking billions of fucked up individuals out there Jackson. In fact, I'm pretty fucked up myself right now, wouldn't you say?
Jack:	Barrie. Straighten up. I love you. Doesn't love count for something?
Barrie:	Love, Jack? People don't love. They don't know how to. The best they can do is try to control things. I can't be controlled, Jack.

People need. They choke each other and think that's love. I don't
know how to say it, but that's what I see, Jack. My mom and dad
do it. They're never really there for each other. Dad seems like
he wants to be somewhere else and Mom always seems like she's
waiting for something to happen. They've stopped seeing each
other. I don't want that to happen to me.

Jack: That's them. This is us. We don't have to live the way other people
           do. We can make it better. What's happening here? How did you
           get here?

Barrie: How the hell are we gonna make a better world? I've done
           drugs my whole life, just to see things in a different light. Acid,
           Schrooms, J.D.. When I come to, it's still the same swirling mass
           of confused campers. No baby, we'll have to find another way.
           We're friends. That's good. Maybe that's the best we can do.

Jack: I want to be a making love to you when they call my number.

Barrie: Thanks, that's real sensitive.

Jack: I just mean…to love each other right to the end. I don't want to go
           limp at sixty and putter around the garage the rest of my life.

Barrie: That's my boy.

Jack: Yeah, I'm your boy. Maybe by the next century, people will be
           able to have simultaneous ascension during orgasm. What do you
           think?

Barrie: I think I like the way you think. You love me, don't you, Jackie?

Jack: Yeah.

Barrie: Not just because I'm funny and can drink you under the table?

Jack: Isn't that enough?

Barrie: I gotta know you love me, Jackie. It's real important you know
           who I am.

Jack: I know who you are and I love you. Why wasn't that enough?

(Jack turns away from her.)

           God! You took her away. I loved her. You do some pretty amazing
           things God, and then you fuck it all up.

(Flashback ends.)

Barrie: What did you know about me? What could you say about Barrie
           that was solid?

Jack: Girl, you were a mystery. But every cell was in its right place when
           we were together. Every bead of sweat, every breath…Nobody
           lived like you did, you left them in the dust. You left me in the dust
           with everyone else.

Barrie: I didn't mean to die. I didn't trust enough. I thought you were an
           illusion, just like me.

Jack: No babe, I was real.

Barrie: I know that now. I came to tell you that I'm sorry, Jackie-boy.

Jack: That's it? You're sorry?

Barrie: I gave in to my delusion. Don't judge your life by my mistake. Live your life, Jack.

Jack: It's not that simple.

Barrie: Yes it is.

Breaking Free

Premise: **He** I am a man, she is a woman; we have a relationship, she is Michael's wife. We are in her apartment. Michael just hit her and knocked her down.

She I am a woman, he is a man; we have a relationship, he is Michael's best friend. We are in my apartment. Michael just hit me and knocked me down.

Jeff: You alright?

Sue: Um, hmm.

Jeff: You're arm okay?

Sue: I'll probably get a hell of a bruise.

Jeff: Jesus. This has got to end.

Sue: Don't say it.

Jeff: This is serious, Sue. Best friend and husband not withstanding, he's the worst kind of prick. I want so bad to put the hurt on him when he pulls this shit.

Sue: He already does hurt. In ways he can't express.

Jeff: Don't make excuses for him with me. I've known him since he was seven.

Sue: It's not an excuse. It's just something I know. He's hurting all the time. I don't think he even knows what makes him so mean. He's like an animal that's been mistreated.

Jeff: You don't deserve it. You don't. You're the one being mistreated.

Sue: Don't.

Jeff: Don't what?

Sue: Give me a speech.

Jeff: I'm sorry. It's none of my business. It's your marriage.

Sue:	I didn't mean…I don't know what I don't mean or what I want to say. I feel ten times more scared right now than when he's in the room.
Jeff:	I'll stay. Or maybe you should leave.
Sue:	Jesus, I'm not ready to think about that.
Jeff:	What's it gonna take, Sue?
Sue:	I don't know. I used to think he just needed an audience. Someone to hear him. It used to be enough. He'd do his show; tell us what is wrong with the world – and with us; get drunk, or more drunk and then calm down.
Jeff:	You mean pass out.
Sue:	You're loaded for bear. What gives?
Jeff:	What gives. What gives is that I can't do this anymore. I can't not tell you how I feel. I can't pretend like I don't know how you feel. This is fuckin' nuts and I don't know what to do exactly, except I know I can't keep doing what I've been doing, which is worse than nothing. I love you, Sue, and I am not going to keep quiet out of respect for your marriage to my fucking best friend who is a god-damned psycho woman hater, because your marriage to that fucker is a dismal tragedy. I know this is not a complete surprise to you. Please, God. Tell me this does not come as a complete surprise to you.
Sue:	You think I want to hear this today. Do you really think I can deal with this right now, at this moment. How much do you think I can handle, Jeff?
Jeff:	You asked. Damn it, you asked and I can't lie about it anymore.
Sue:	Another day, another week. You could have lied, just one more time, you've done it plenty. You're good at it. Why today, Jeff? Why now?
Jeff:	Sue. Sue, I'm sorry. You don't have to do anything. I just told you how I feel. I didn't say you had to do anything. I don't expect you to do anything.
Sue:	Oh, but I do, I do have to do something, because now you've said it. Now we can't pretend anymore. Now you've busted the whole thing wide open and I have to do something because I can't face Michael now. Now I can't ever be in the same damn room with him because he'll know. He'll know it's you and me against him. His worst fears will be confirmed and he will kill me. In fact, why don't you just kill me now and get it over with. Go ahead. Just strangle me or stab me or something. Do it, Jeff. Quick! Before he comes back. Be quick and merciful. Because he won't. He'll torture me. Long drawn out torture. The kind he's best at. God damn it, why did you have to tell me this now?

Jeff:	It's not getting better, Sue. Isn't that what we were hoping for? That it would get better. It's getting worse. You just said it yourself. He's capable of killing you and the only reason he doesn't is that he enjoys torturing you more. I said it because you're not safe and he's not my friend. I stopped loving him a year ago. I've been pretending so that I could be around. To make sure he didn't do anything really bad. But we saw it today. Me being here doesn't make any difference anymore. He hit you hard enough to knock you down. I think he knows it hurts you more when someone else is around and sees it. He takes pleasure in that. It's sadistic.
Sue:	I don't know what is real anymore. I thought I knew why you're always around. Or at least I hoped I did, but I'm so scared. Sometimes I'm sure I'm kidding myself; a way to have hope where there is no hope. I've been thinking I'm losing my mind, Jeff. I was too afraid to think you really love me. I'm so ashamed that my life got to be this way.
Jeff:	You have nothing to be ashamed of. My god, we both loved him so we feel guilty that we don't. Even more guilty that we have feelings for each other—that we have in some way betrayed Michael. I let that doubt keep me quiet for too long.
Sue:	Well, you sure fixed that.
Jeff:	I wasn't misreading you?
Sue:	No, you read me right, but honestly my feelings are very fucked up. I have this unreasonable fear, like something horrible is about to happen. I want to scream and run for the hills and at the same time laugh and fall down and hug you and kiss you…but this is probably some syndrome, that prisoners get when they're about to be executed, I think. Like Ann Boleyn right before King Henry had her beheaded. I'm nuts, I'm sorry. What, what, what are we supposed to do now? I'm babbling. But I really feel like I gotta get out of here. He's gonna come back. To make sure I'm not talking to anybody.
Jeff:	Okay, here's what we'll do. You're right. You should not be here. And neither should I. In fact we should be together, don't you think? I think so. So we'll go to the lake. We'll have time to think…talk…to figure this out.
Sue:	Is anybody else there?
Jeff:	No.
Sue:	Okay, that's a plan.
Jeff:	Get some stuff.
Sue:	Stuff…
Jeff:	Now. Please…Let's get out of here.

Sue:	Okay...only need a few things. No, nothing. I need nothing. Let's just go.
Jeff:	Good. Very good thinking. Christ, I'm gonna have an anxiety attack.
Sue:	We can take the stairs. He'll take the elevator.
Jeff:	Fuck him. I don't care if we run into him.
Sue:	I do.
Jeff:	Yes, of course you do. Okay...to the lake. We're going to the lake. We'll be okay there – we'll think...we'll figure this out.
Sue:	*(She stops; looks around the apartment.)*
Jeff:	I promise you. We're doing the right thing.

(They leave.)

Don't Make Me Over

Premise: **He** I am a man, she is a woman; we have a relationship, I don't know what it is; I don't know where we are.

She I am a woman, he is a man; we have a relationship, I don't know what it is; I don't know where we are.

Sheldon: Wow! Punky, you look great.

Punky: My hair cut? I don't know. Techno mishap if you ask me.

Sheldon: You're funny. Tilt-a-whirl, man.

Punky: Don't tease me, Sheldon.

Sheldon: I'm serious. I think your humor is total.

Punky: C'mon, we'll be late.

Sheldon: Did you change your make-up? You got that sheen, that shine… aluminum piston.

Punky: Do you really like it?

Sheldon: I love it. You really know how to put it on. It's turbine, totally turbine. I feel real jack when I'm with you.

Punky: Shelly, you're gonna make me fuse out.

Sheldon: I'm serious. You really lay it down.

Punky: Lay off it, Sheldon. I can't snake with this.

Sheldon: Believe me. I'm layin' down a straight line. You are fuel injected.

Punky: I wish you wouldn't vibe that way on me.

Sheldon: God, Punky! Why are you so alloyed out on yourself? I mean you really can't snake a pow fume can you?

Punky: It's not a vertical thing for me. I mean I'm really about as un-total as a girl could be. And when you flash me like that, I feel like I'm puttin' you through a bad roll.

Sheldon: What's the juice? How come your self-image is all splinters?

Punky:	Your cones aren't perkin' on the real thing.
Sheldon:	I'm not tracin'. What are you puttin' down?
Punky:	To begin with I had a nose job when I was twelve. My parents told me I had a devoted scepter and it needed to be fixed.
Sheldon:	A devoted scepter? Am I sand? What's that?
Punky:	Oh, hell it was something like that, I can never remember. Made me whistle when I breathed.
Sheldon:	You mean a deviated septum. The middle part of your nose.
Punky:	You got the blaze.
Sheldon:	So what… so you had a nose job. A lot of people need them. It's a little archaic, but you get the quiet airflow now, right?
Punky:	They told me that after the operation, my nose might look a little different, but it would still be my nose. When they took the bandages off it looked different. They said it takes a couple of months for the swelling to go down, so it wouldn't look normal for a while. I waited. I didn't even look in the mirror. The swelling went down but my nose never checked back in.
Sheldon:	D.U. What a flame. No gassin', the nose is sonic.
Punky:	I just wish it was mine.
Sheldon:	It is now.
Punky:	When I was thirteen they said I needed skin surgery. They said I had some unusual dark spots that should be removed. I thought they were just freckles then. I guess they were really moles. There were two on my stomach, one on my neck and two on my face, so off they went. My mother started acting different towards me after that. Took me shopping with her and to the stylist. I had my first tint when I was fourteen. Mom said my hair needed a little more pizzazz. Pizzazz…what a bronzed expression.
Sheldon:	Hey baby, you're jet. Believe me. Don't worry about your bronzed mom.
Punky:	That wasn't the end of it. When I was fifteen my mom says, "We girls are taking a little vacation"…Palm Springs. It's Easter weekend, so I figure I'll most likely be able to wrap it. Nice warp, you know.
Sheldon:	You're ripping my lining. I can't stand the thought of you in a hub with some frame from Orange County.
Punky:	Just listen, will you? I'm thinking it'll be the standard rustle right? Well, we check into a place that looks like someone's house, and I say, "What's the band?" Mom says, "This is Doctor Pulare's Spa and Clinic". I spent five days lying by his pool waiting for the tucks in my butt to heal. I was in primary meltdown. I told my mother, "If you didn't like the deal, why didn't you turn me

around? Get a better kid?" And then she said, "We only want you to be happy. When we adopted you we decided you were going to get the best of everything." That's when I went into final, irreversible, psychic fusion.

Sheldon: Don't get so peeled. So your mother is pinched. That's her window.

Punky: That was the first I'd heard that I was adopted. She forgot they hadn't told me. After that Dad left her. Don't you see? I wasn't what they wanted so they just kept trying to make me over into something they could hang with.

Sheldon: Punky, like I said before; to me you're jet, you're blazin'. Be with me. Together we'll deep a superstructure like no one has ever fabricated, not in their archest ripple.

Punky: Retract the laser beam. I'm tryin' to tell you how I feel.

Sheldon: Blazin'.

Punky: Right now it's kinda cold steel and echoes.

Sheldon: You zappin' me?

Punky: No – I just need it to groove in the soil for a while. No hazmats.

Sheldon: So I'm still in orbit?

Punky: Of course. I couldn't snake these waves if you weren't holdin' the gyro.

Sheldon: You had me exxo-terminatin'.

Punky: No man, your current's good.

Don't Cry

Premise: **He** I am a man, she is a woman; we have a relationship, she is my mother. We are in her hospital room.

She I am a woman, he is a man; we have a relationship, he is my son. We are in my hospital room.

John:	Hey, how ya doin'?
Laura:	Pretty good for the shape I'm in.
John:	Brought you some magazines. And what else? Oh, cinnamon candies. You'll need a fire hose to cool your mouth after y' eat these.
Laura:	Johnny, you spoil me rotten.
John:	Just encouragin' you to get better faster.
Laura:	I swear you should be a doctor. You got the healin' gift.
John:	Get outta here.
Laura:	In your heart you do.
John:	Ma…
Laura:	I didn't mean to embarrass you. Things just pop outta my mouth these days. Don't think about it too much. Just comes out. Whatever I'm thinkin'.
John:	It's okay, Ma, you been through a lot. Your mind'll clear up real soon now. More familiar surroundings, the things you like to eat. Those thing'll bring you right back.
Laura:	You think so?
John:	Sure as I know anything.
Laura:	Johnny boy, I need to tell you something'. Sit close here, will ya?
John:	I know we're almost outta money, Ma. I got a plan. I'm gonna re-enlist. I don't need to go to school right away. We just need to get

you home and on your feet, then I'll sign up. You can take your time getting well and I'll send you my pay. I don't need much livin' on a damn boat. Sorry to cuss.

Laura: John, be still now.

John: Alright, miss bossy.

Laura: God help me, but you take the starch outta me with your sass. Honey, don't interrupt me for a minute. What I got to say is important for you to hear.

John: Okay, you da boss.

Laura: I won't be comin' home, honey. The cancer is progressin' too fast. The doctor told me this morning, but I didn't need him to tell me, I knew. I been knowin' for a few days now.

John: How do you know? You don't know for sure.

Laura: Don't interrupt me. My energy is goin'. I want you to know that it's alright with me. I'm not afraid of goin'. I'd like to be here an' see you get married someday. Meet my grandchirren. But that's not what God has in mind. And it's okay. Now I don't want you re-enlistin'. I want you to use your benefits and go to school just like you were plannin' afore I took sick.

John: Ma, you're startin' to talk country. What's the matter with you? You sound like ol' granny Haig.

Laura: Stop interruptin'. I know you's upset honey, but I'm tired now. I worked hard talkin' good English whilst you was growin' up, so's you'd learn good and have a future. But, my God, it took a lot of energy. Feels good to jus' relax an' let it come the way is natch'l to me.

John: Ma, cut it out. You on some new drug or somethin'? What's the matter with you?

Laura: Nothin' much the matter with me now, darlin', 'cept I'm dyin'. That's what I'm tryin' to tell you. I don't want you cryin' 'bout what I did or didn't have in my life. I had everthin' that mattered to me. I had yo Daddy just as long as God was willin' to let me keep him. And I have you. It's enough for me John. I want you to know that, 'cause I want you to go on with your life with no regret.

John: How can I not regret it when I know what you've done your whole life with no damn help from God.

Laura: John.

John: Only thing about you God ever noticed was what he could take away from you. Daddy, a good home, a chance for a day of rest and peace. What the hell kind of a God are we talkin' about. How can you say you've had enough when you haven't had enough for as long as I can remember?

Laura: Thass just it, honey, you only members yo life. You cain't
          'member all o'mine. I never wanted much, so I never needed
          much. I had a wonnerfull husbind, a beautiful boy, that's what I
          ast God for when I was old enough to think fo' myseff. God gave
          me jus' what I ast fo'. An he gon' give you jus' what you ask fo'.
          That's why I tellin' you this.

John: What about me? I didn't ask God to take my daddy and I sure as
          hell didn't ask him to take you. You an' God gonna just make a
          deal and leave me out of it?

Laura: Jes' the opposite. You the heart of this, baby. God an' me we want
          you to have a life, so he's takin' me into his care so you can be
          free, honey, to live yo' life. God don't want you takin' care some
          broken down ol' thing. He want you fine yourseff a beautiful
          young thing to make a life with. Study, get th' 'tunity you lookin'
          fo'. I tire't now honey. Hol' my han'. Tha's nice. Lucky woman I
          am.

John: Ma. Sorry I sassed you. I just don't understand your attitude about
          God. Don't you ever get angry? Damn it Mama, talk to me. Sorry
          for cussin'. Mama. Mama? Oh, man. Ma, it's Johnny boy, wake
          up. Ain't you got another word to say to me? I love you, ma. You
          know that, don't you? I love you with all my heart an' soul. You
          tell God he's got some answerin' to do when he meets me face to
          face.

Düsseldorf

Premise: **He** I am a man, she is a woman; we have a relationship, we used to be lovers. We are in a train station. I haven't seen her since Belgrade.

                She I am a woman, he is a man; we have a relationship, we used to be lovers. We are in a train station. I haven't seen him since Belgrade.

She:	Fredrich.
He:	Johanna. You're the last person I expected to see traveling today.
She:	I might say the same about you.
He:	We didn't have much of a goodbye in Belgrade. I knew some day I'd have to explain myself.
She:	Please. Don't say anything.
He:	But I want you to understand.
She:	Shhh. Time will tell us more than we can tell each other right now. And besides, it's New Year's Day. A day for new beginnings.
He:	New beginnings. That's what we're best at, you and I. Isn't it?
She:	Which train are you headed for?
He:	The morning express to Vienna.
She:	I didn't know the express ran on holidays?
He:	Yes. Always.
She:	I didn't know.
He:	And you? Where to?
She:	Zurich.
He:	Zurich. We had a fine time in Zurich, didn't we?
She:	Your clothes are rumpled. Did you travel overnight?
He:	Yes. From Madrid.
She:	Alone.

He:	Quite.
She:	How unlike you. And on New Year's Eve.
He:	Zurich. In Zurich you danced for me at the flower mart just before dawn.
She:	No, that was London. Covent Garden.
He:	London was it?
She:	They're calling my train.
He:	Is there a number where I can reach you?
She:	Fredrich, we've never communicated by phone. I wouldn't know how to behave.
He:	So much happened in Belgrade. So much you couldn't have known.
She:	We each have our tears, my darling. Belgrade was Belgrade. We may confuse London with Zurich, maybe even Vienna, but I will always remember Düsseldorf. Won't you?
He:	Johanna.
She:	I'll miss my train. Happy New Year, Fredrich.
He:	Happy New Year. I remember Düsseldorf.
She:	Do you Fredrich?
He:	Always.
She:	Then Düsseldorf is ours forever. Au revoir.
He:	Adieu.

Evelyn

Premise: **Jack** I am a man, she is a woman; we're meeting for the first time. We are on the campus of the college/university that we both attend.

Evelyn I am a woman, he is a man; we're meeting for the first time. We are on the campus of the college/university that we both attend.

Evelyn:	Jack Kimble?
Jack:	Yes?
Evelyn:	Hi.
Jack:	Hi.
Evelyn:	I'm Evelyn Orisman.
Jack:	Hi.
Evelyn:	Hi. I like your column. Well. That's not completely true. Can I ask you a question?
Jack:	I don't know. Can you?
Evelyn:	How come you write your poetry under the name J.P. South?
Jack:	How do you know about that?
Evelyn:	I really like your poetry. I wanted to meet you. I don't mean I don't think your column is good, I'm just not into campus politics.
Jack:	Thanks.
Evelyn:	How'd you get your own column? You're not a senior.
Jack:	Anything else you want to tell me about myself?
Evelyn:	I'm sorry. Do you mind me saying all this? Are you a journalism major?
Jack:	Can I answer one at a time please?
Evelyn:	I'm sorry. Yes, of course.

Jack:	In reverse order the answers are: "Not exactly", "No", and "Eastman liked an editorial I wrote". It's no big deal. It's not exactly the New York Times. How come you like my poetry?
Evelyn:	It's incredible. It doesn't feel like a young man's poetry. It's so expansive, soulful. It's like you know the same things I know. It touches me.
Jack:	No kidding?
Evelyn:	You don't think I sound like an idiot?
Jack:	No, it's great. What's your major?
Evelyn:	Philosophy.
Jack;	Hmmm.
Evelyn:	What does that mean?
Jack:	It scares me. Philosophy.
Evelyn:	What do you mean? Your poetry is philosophic.
Jack:	No. The study of philosophy scares me. You start lining up someone's ideals into a particular school of philosophy, it distorts it. Limits it.
Evelyn:	It's just a way to organize the information. It's really fun. Studying all the different philosophers opens me up to consider what I believe myself.
Jack:	Well, that's good, if you can do it. I mean, know what you believe that's different from what everybody else believes.
Evelyn:	Maybe we all really believe the same things.
Jack:	That's too frightening to even think about.
Evelyn:	Well, how is it we can understand what someone's telling us even if we've never thought about it before?
Jack:	Because we have intelligence. Philosophy is different; it comes from direct experience. Philosophers write from experience.
Evelyn:	Or inspiration, and we get the significance even though we're not them.
Jack:	Reading a book isn't experience, it's voyeurism.
Evelyn:	Then why do philosophers write? And why do millions of people read them?
Jack:	Well it's provocative; makes you think. But it's dangerous to take someone else's experience and not have one of your own. Without the direct experience, it can never be more than an idea, a thought. Thought is too static.
Evelyn:	Why do you write?
Jack:	Trying to comprehend. When I write, a space opens up in front of me, draws me in…

Evelyn:	Keeps opening up…
Both:	Drawing me further from myself.
Evelyn:	"Conscious Fall", that's a great poem.
Jack:	You really know my stuff, huh?
Evelyn:	Only what I've read.
Jack:	There's more where that came from.
Evelyn:	I'd love to read it sometime.
Jack:	Okay. Do you think other people talk like this?
Evelyn:	Sure. All over the world.
Jack:	I mean ordinary people. I never hear my parents talk about these things. Do you?
Evelyn:	Yes. My parents are very thoughtful people.
Jack:	So are mine. They just think about other things. I don't know. This is all new to me. I know there's another way of understanding that's more vital. It has to do with the direct experience. I haven't had it yet, but I have such a strong feeling it's right there. Almost within my reach.
Evelyn:	Like starlight?
Jack:	Huh?
Evelyn:	What we see is the light, not the star. We never see the star itself. We know it's there. We take it on faith.
Jack:	We know the moon is there. We can see it, walk on it even. But what I want to know is how the hell did it get there?
Evelyn:	Someday we'll know. Probably already know and just can't remember.
Jack:	Maybe.
Evelyn:	You should take a philosophy course.
Jack:	No thanks. I start reading that stuff and my mind wanders. An hour goes by and I'm still reading the same paragraph.
Evelyn:	Maybe you could start with something light.
Jack:	Maybe in grad school. You got a boyfriend?
Evelyn:	Nope. How about you?
Jack:	Nope. No boyfriend.
Evelyn:	Wise guy. You know what I meant.
Jack:	Someone steady? Yes and no. I've dated this girl since high school. She loves me. Wants to marry me, but I don't think she really knows who I am. She considers my writing and my poetry a hobby and keeps asking me if I've chosen a major yet.
Evelyn:	What's her name?

Jack: Adriana.

Evelyn: Have you told her how you feel?

Jack: No. I'm avoiding it. I don't want to hurt her. She has so many plans for us. I just don't see my future as clearly as she does. It disturbs me that she's counting on me so much.

Evelyn: Do you believe in destiny?

Jack: I'd like to know I have a purpose in life.

Evelyn: I believe you have an appointment with destiny, Jack. Some people will understand that. Some just don't. You're so gifted. I feel that I already know so much about you. I'm glad we met, aren't you?

Jack: Pretty direct.

Evelyn: I'm a philosophy major.

Jack: Are all philosophy majors so sure of themselves?

Evelyn: Are all poets great lovers?

Jack: So the story goes.

Faith and Passion

Premise: **He** I am a man, she is a woman; we have a relationship, we work together. We are in my office.

She I am a woman, he is a man; we have a relationship, we work together. He is the Reverend Father. We are in his office.

He: Sister. It's good to see you.

She: Don't be polite.

He: I am glad to see you.

She: Martin. This is an uncomfortable moment.

He: Yes. Mary, can we talk as friends? As man and woman?

She: I would rather not.

(He looks at her for a moment)

She: Just, not right now.

He: When?

She: This place… The people... It always felt right. I belonged…I… why are you looking at me that way?

He: This place hasn't changed so dramatically.

She: No, but the experience is different now.

He: Your work here? The people. No longer important to you?

She: That's not what I'm saying.

He: And your faith?

She: Martin, don't ask me that.

He: I'm asking you.

She: Please, Martin.

He: I asked you a question.

She:	Are you asking as my friend or boss?
He:	If I ask you as a friend, will you answer me?
She:	Maybe this has all been a mistake. Maybe I've been hiding here to avoid myself. There's a lot you don't know.
He:	Whether you go or stay, we are friends at this moment. Please respect that.
She:	Martin…I have broken my vows. I have been with a man.
He:	I was afraid I was going to have to say it.
She:	You knew?
He:	Not for sure. He must be quite a man.
She:	Oh lord no! He's no kind of man. I mean, he is a man. A certain type of man.
He:	Are you in love?
She:	No. He's just the perfect type to shred all of one's moral fiber. The wounded animal type. Sucks you right in.
He:	Why are you leaving?
She:	I can't stay here now. It would be a fraud.
He:	Alright, so you've slept with a man.
She:	What?
He:	Do you think that makes any difference to a person like Pat Reilly? If it weren't for you, he'd be…God knows where he'd be.
She:	Please. Don't do that.
He:	Is this the first time in your life you've done something you've regretted?
She:	This is not a small regret.
He:	Welcome to the real world. These walls are only plaster and wood. They won't keep out stray thoughts and impulses. We are in the service of God, Mary, but we are human beings. I should think your greater sin is coveting some idea of a perfect record.
She:	Don't complicate this, Martin.
He:	I can't stop you. But I would suggest that before you burn your bridges, you take a sabbatical. Give yourself time to think.
She:	It can never be the same.
He:	Of course it'll never be the same. You've been with a man now. You hadn't before, but tomorrow would have been different from today anyway. Look at what you have gained and weigh it against what you think you've lost. You are a gifted person with deep roots in the parish. It would be a tragic loss to us all if you left without being sure why.

She:	I am sure.
He:	You are only sure of your shock and your chagrin, right now. But that will change.
She:	What makes you so sure?
He:	Do you know why I became a priest?
She:	Is this a trick question?
He:	Because I had great self-loathing and a huge fear.
She:	Why?
He:	Because I'm homosexual. I thought by being a priest I could make up for this horrible defect and thought I could hide from it. I wouldn't have to get married and have a family and I could be a part of society instead of the freak I thought I was.
She:	I am so sorry, Martin.
He:	For what?
She:	That you would feel that way about yourself.
He:	You're not shocked – not made uncomfortable by that knowledge?
She:	How could I be? You're my friend – you're certainly not a freak.
He:	That's my point – neither are you.
She:	You had the forgivable uncertainty of youth.
He:	It didn't feel that way at the time. Turns out I made a very good decision for all the wrong reasons. On the positive side, I sought refuge in the seminary and I found my center and discovered my strengths. I don't regret it. In fact I've been thrilled by life. At times I've indulged in some heavy bouts of pride as well.
She:	Good for you. You deserve it.
He:	I'm not sure I know where I'm going with this, but can I say one more thing?
She:	Please do.
He:	I'm worried that you might be doing to yourself what I did when I was young…hating yourself for exploring your own nature. If that's what's pushing you out the door, please reconsider.
She:	Tell me we're not deeply deluded, Martin. I need something to believe in right now.
He:	You have the right to know yourself, and the responsibility as well, really. You can't judge how and when these moments come.
She:	Boy, is that true.
He:	I will confess, my advice is laced with self-interest. I don't want you to leave.
She:	Thank you Martin.

George Died

Premise: **He** I am a man, she is a woman; we have a relationship, she is my wife. We are in our home. George died.

She I am a woman, he is a man; we have a relationship, he is my husband. We are in our home.

Mike: Jan called. Just got word from San Jose. George died.

Rosie: George? Our George?

Mike: Yeah, our George. Jan said he had a heart attack.

Rosie: Jan? She doesn't even know him.

Mike: Someone called the office. She took the call.

Rosie: Poor Hazel.

Mike: Poor George.

Rosie: We should go up.

Mike: I don't know.

Rosie: You don't know what?

Mike: If I can… it's …I don't know. I'm having a little trouble with this.

Rosie: It's a shock.

Mike: It's a fucking waste.

Rosie: I'd like to think he's in a better place now.

Mike: What better place? His wife and kids are here. He lived for them. They are everything to him.

Rosie: Do you think there's a bigger picture? I mean a grand scheme? I feel there is.

Mike: Yeah, and in the grand scheme of things George got rooked.

Rosie: Mike.

Mike:	To be ripped from your kids. How can there be anything good in that. He doesn't get to see them grow up, to see who they will become. They don't have him when they need him.
Rosie:	It's a tragedy…for all of them. Why are you taking this so personally?
Mike:	It's not fair. He never hurt anybody. His kids don't deserve this.
Rosie:	I agree, but why are you so angry?
Mike:	I don't get it.
Rosie:	What's to get? It's a shock and a great loss. Look, I think we'll feel better if we do something. I'm gonna call Hazel's sister and see what I can find out. You call Mary and see if Aiden can take care of the dog. Honey?
Mike:	It's my grandfather. It's my god-damned grandfather. He's still fuckin' with me.
Rosie:	What?
Mike:	He was an ugly, spoiled, mean, son-of-a-bitch drunk, and he lived for fuckin' ever. He didn't even like being alive and he lived to be 98. And a guy like George, who loves life, dies at 46. That's what I don't get.
Rosie:	This is about your grandfather?
Mike:	Yes. Every time a young person dies, I think—"Why couldn't that have happened to him?" My mother's life would have been a hell of a lot better.
Rose:	But your mother never says a thing about him that would indicate…
Mike:	My mother has rewritten history her whole life, which included bribing us so we wouldn't tell Dad about the shit my grandfather did.
Rosie:	What sort of things?
Mike:	Hitting my mother. Belittling her. Smashing my head against the tile wall in the bathroom. Passing out drunk on more than one lawn.
Rosie:	Jesus, Mike. How come you kept all this in?
Mike:	For Mom. She can't help it. She needs to remember him as a good father.
Rosie:	I can't believe I never knew this. You guys, I mean no one… everyone seems… Do Jack and Don feel the same way?
Mike:	Yes—in fact for Jack it's even worse. He saw some stuff he won't talk about.
Rosie:	Did you all agree to never discuss it?

Mike:	No, it's an unspoken deal. It just evolved. We got very good at going on as if nothing was happening. Never knew when he would go off on her or how long it would last.
Rosie:	I'm so sorry. And a little amazed that I'm just hearing this now.
Mike:	Every family has its weirdnesses.
Rosie:	We don't have to go to San Jose, if it's too hard for you.
Mike:	No. I want to go. I won't let him get in the way of my own life. I promised myself that. What are you looking at?
Rosie:	You. You look different to me.
Mike:	Shocked? All this ugliness in me?
Rosie:	Not at all. You look sort of noble and innocent.
Mike:	I have never felt very innocent.
Rosie:	You were. Before the nightmare started...before, during and after. It's not your fault your grandfather was so screwed up.
Mike:	I've always felt guilty for not protecting my mother better.
Rosie:	It wasn't your job.
Mike:	God, Rosie, I love you. I don't know what I'd do if anything ever happened to you.
Rosie:	Hopefully you'll never have to find out. It's scary, isn't it? George dying.
Mike:	Yeah.

Kingdom Come

Premise: **He** I am a man, she is a woman; we are meeting for the first time. We are at MGM Studios.

She I am Bella, he is a man; we are meeting for the first time. We are at the threshold of a new beginning.

Bella: Surrender all ye who enter here.

Steve: Excuse me?

Bella: There is no excuse. No good excuse anyway.

Steve: Forgive me, I must be in the…

Bella: You are forgiven. We are all forgiven. There is no act against the universe that causes lasting damage, at least nothing you could do. So you are forgiven for thinking that anything you do matters. You pompous ass.

Steve: Who are you?

Bella: Who are you?

Steve: I asked you first.

Bella: Only according to your method of time sequencing. Surrender!

Steve: Surrender? To what?

Bella: You ask far too many questions.

Steve: Look, I have an appointment with Mr. Mayer. This is MGM isn't it? Where is Mr. Mayer's office?

Bella: There is no Mr. Mayer. You are about sixty human years too late.

Steve: What?

Bella: There you go again. Questions, questions, questions. Surrender!

Steve: Look lady, I'm sorry if you didn't get the part, but I have an appointment with Mr. Mayer, so cut the act and let me in.

Bella: Impertinent little mortal.

Steve:	I don't believe this. Are you for real?
Bella:	Real? Now, that's a relative thing.
Steve:	Just let me in, huh?
Bella:	You must believe to enter here. This is a place of magic. Your friend, Mr. Mayer, created it to be that way. He saw what was happening.
Steve:	In entertainment?
Bella:	Chronic self-importance of pandemic proportions.
Steve:	You're a hoot.
Bella:	It all started with the "pitch". Self-serving. Pathetic really. Then it was the "deal". Such a deal. Led to mayhem.
Steve:	You're really an actor, right? Who put you up to this?
Bella:	Your name is Steven Sapperstein, but you go by the name Steve Sharp. You were born in the Bronx; parents of German descent. You worked with the "Voice of America", where a number of creative and compassionate souls sought to bring hope to the embattled people of Europe. One of your colleagues told you you had promise as an actor and referred you to Mr. Mayer. Much has occurred since you boarded the train in New York, Mr. Sapperstein.
Steve:	How do you know all this about me? Not even Mr. Mayer knew all this. I was working on a new resume on the train.
Bella:	Don't be alarmed. This now serves as the control center for the re-alignment project.
Steve:	There is no Mr. Mayer?
Bella:	No.
Steve:	But I'm here. And you're expecting me.
Bella:	Your gift will now be able to reach an audience larger than your wildest dreams. It is more powerful than even Mr. Mayer's magic silver screen.
Steve:	New technology?
Bella:	You don't get it, do you?
Steve:	What?
Bella:	It's dimensional. Not technical.
Steve:	I'm still on the train and I'm dreaming?
Bella:	Sort of. You've traveled out of time. The things you wish to accomplish are…It's better that they be initiated outside time and space.
Steve:	So? What? I'm at an inter-dimensional doorway?

Bella: Yes! And all you need to do is trust. Surrender and let go. The rest will come clear to you.

Steve: That's good. I'm looking forward to that. What's your name?

Bella: Bella.

Steve: Bella. It's beautiful here, Bella.

Bella: Si, Bella. Molte bella.

Land of the Free

Premise: **He** I am a man, she is a woman; we have a relationship, I don't know what it is. We are in the diner where she works.

She I am a woman, he is a man; we have a relationship, he is one of my regulars. We are in the diner where I work.

Rosie: More coffee, Baker?

Baker: Thanks, Rosie. Where's the boss today?

Rosie: He'll be in. How was breakfast?

Baker: Good. As usual. Rosa.

Rosie: What'd you say?

Baker: Rosa bella.

Rosie: Rosie is my name.

Baker: I have this theory that when a girl goes to work in a diner, she changes her name. Rosie is a very popular name in diners.

Rosie: That's a very funny idea. Why would a girl, a woman, change her name?

Baker: So some lovesick customer couldn't find out where she lives and surprise her one night.

Rosie: Not a bad reason. That girl might be pretty smart.

Baker: Or, because her boss makes all the girls change their names.

Rosie: That would be a bad reason. I'm named for my grandmother. Her name was Rose.

Baker: Where are you from?

Rosie: I am an American.

Baker: Your gramma too? My parents came from South Africa. Originally.

Rosie: I am an American. That's all. Please, I gotta get back to work.

Baker:	Where are your people from?
Rosie:	Forget it. It's not important.
Baker:	It is to me.
Rosie:	Why?
Baker:	I'm curious.
Rosie:	You're a pain in the ass.
Baker:	Careful.
Rosie:	Get lost, Baker. You're ruining my day.
Baker:	C'mon Rosie.
Rosie:	Buzz off.
Baker:	Rosie, I can help you.
Rosie:	Baker please, leave me alone.
Baker:	I met a man from Managua. He's here looking for some of his family. He thinks they've been indentured by the people who helped them come here. He can't trace them at all. The postcards he got just said, "We are fine. Life here is good." no return address. It's pretty hard to believe, slavery in this day and age.
Rosie:	You want to get me killed?
Baker:	Just tell me how he got you here. Where you came from. Your name. I'll do the rest.
Rosie:	If they discover you, we're both dead.
Baker:	Just give me the information.
Rosie:	My name is Isabella Constancia. I'm from the Valle De Los Aguillas. It's a province in the west. In Columbia. He took us by boat at night to Ensinadas, in Mexico. Then by car. We came through just east of San Diego, an old stage road. The fence moves. They pay the patrols.
Baker:	Alright. I'll come in a few more times. I won't know anything. Just treat me the same as usual. Then I'll be gone for about a month. You must remain calm even if you don't hear from me.
Rosie:	Why are you doin' this?
Baker:	The less you know, the better. You're too good for this place Rosie. Remember that.
Rosie:	Yeah, yeah, yeah. And you're John Wayne.
Baker:	You never know.
Rosie:	For God's sake, be careful, Baker.
Baker:	Count on it.

Let's Dance

Premise: **He** I am a man, she is a woman; we have a relationship, she is my wife. We are in our home.

She I am a woman, he is a man; we have a relationship, he is my husband. We are in our home.

He: Let's go dancing.

She: Should we?

He: Of course we should, It's Saturday night and we haven't gone out in ages.

She: I was going to finish my sewing tonight.

He: Oh, c'mon! You can sew any night of the week. Let's go. I really feel like dancing.

She: I've got class two nights this week, plus we're supposed to have dinner with Pete and Alice.

He: Okay, so you can sew next week, c'mon. How 'bout it? Huh? What d'ya say. It'll be like a date.

She: I don't have anything to wear.

He: You have a closet, no, two closets full of clothes. How can you not have anything to wear? How 'bout the sexy T-shirt dress with the slit up the side. You look great in it.

She: It's dirty.

He: How can it be dirty? We haven't been out in months. I can't remember the last time I saw you in it.

She: Well, it's got a spot on it so I can't wear it.

He: Too bad. Wear one of your other ones.

She: They're too long. I've got to take them up.

He: Why don't you want to go out? Are you mad at me?

She: Not yet. I just don't feel like going out. I had planned to stay in and get caught up on work.

He:	Pooper.
She:	Ricky. Don't make me feel bad. If I played every time you wanted to I'd never get anything done.
He:	Well if you don't play with me sometimes I'm going to go stark raving mad. Mad, do you hear? Crazed. You catch my drift. How come you never want to go out?
She:	I like to go out. After the work is done then I feel like I can give myself a treat.
He:	Treat-schmeat. How 'bout just going out for the hell of it. Just to have fun. You don't have to earn every moment of fun in life, you know.
She:	I know that. I'm just worried about having enough money, that's all.
He:	What good is money if all you can do is worry about it? Loosen up, kid. Enjoy life.
She:	Alright joy-boy. Who's going to pay the bills?
He:	The bills will get paid. We get 'em paid.
She:	Just in the nick of time.
He:	Come on, I'm bored. I want to go dancing.
She:	Do you think I'm boring?
He:	I didn't say you're boring, I said I am bored. That's different.
She:	I knew we shouldn't live together. I knew you'd get bored with me. We should have kept separate apartments.
He:	Susie! We're married. Married people live together.
She:	Not all of them.
He:	No, just the ones who can't afford a divorce.
She:	Divorce. Do you want a divorce? Is that what you're telling me? Now you want a divorce. Great!
He:	Someone left her sense of humor at the office.
She:	Divorce isn't funny.
He:	I don't want a divorce. I want to go dancing.
She:	Well, you sure have a funny way of asking.
He:	Will you go?
She:	What'll I wear?
He:	Your pink dress. I love your pink dress.
She:	No.
He:	What?
She:	I don't have shoes to go with it.
He:	What did you used to wear with it, galoshes?

She:	Fun-nee. The heel broke on my Guccis.
He:	How about the metallic, kind of shimmery one.
She:	It needs a belt with it.
He:	Didn't a belt come with it?
She:	Yeah, but it's all wrong. Cheap patent.
He:	Well, can't you wear it without the belt?
She:	God no!
He:	You can wear the designer dress you mother sent you and your new black heels.
She:	I can't.
He:	Why?
She:	I haven't gotten stockings to go with it yet. Besides, the shoes pinch my toes. I couldn't dance in them.
He:	Maybelle, we're stuck like a flivver in the mud.
She:	Don't call me Maybelle.
He:	You're acting like Maybelle.
She:	Shut up.
He:	Maybelle, the shut-in. Died with a closet full of beautiful clothes. People always wondered about Mayb…
She:	Asshole.
He:	Why is this so hard?
She:	I don't want to go out with you. You're mean.
He:	I didn't start out mean. I was once a mild mannered reporter.
She:	You're a dingbat.
He:	She loves me, ladies and gentlemen. Only a woman who loves deeply calls her man a dingbat.
She:	You are.
He:	I know. It's you. You make me nutty.
She:	No way.
He:	You want some popcorn?
She:	Popcorn?
He:	Let's watch *Casablanca* and fall in love all over again.
She:	Okay, okay, okay, the sewing can wait.

Metaphysically Absurd

Premise: **He** I am a man, she is a woman; we have a relationship, she is my wife. We are in our home. I just copped some LSD.

She I am a woman, he is a man; we have a relationship, he is my husband. We are in our home.

Brett: Hi, doodle bug.

Crispin: Brett, please don't call me that okay? It's such a bummer, I mean; to realize that to you, my essence is merely a doodle bug kind of a thing is, well…really kind of depressing.

Brett: How do you think I came up with it in the first place?

Crispin: Probably a bad mushroom.

Brett: Crispin… Come on. It's an endearment. It means I love you.

Crispin: Then say you love me. What's so hard about that. Must everything be a metaphor? An "As if"?

Brett: Okay, okay, okay. That's brilliant. God, you're so connected for a Catholic.

Crispin: Don't change the subject.

Brett: What's the subject?

Crispin: A simple straight-forward "I love you".

Brett: I love you.

Crispin: Thank you. And stop calling me a Catholic. I am not a Catholic. I was raised as a Catholic, but I have chosen to be nothing – just like you. You were raised Methodist, but I don't call you Methodist, so please don't call me a Catholic.

Brett: Jesus, have you been makin' a list or something?

Crispin: No. It just bugs me the way you label me. Doodle bug – Catholic.

Brett:	I wasn't calling you a Catholic. That's not what I meant. I meant that you are very highly evolved in spite of your Catholic upbringing.
Crispin:	The subtlety of the distinction is artistic at least.
Brett:	You're hip, honey, truly hip, I mean it. I brought you a little after dinner treat.
Crispin:	Yeah? What?
Brett:	It's a surprise. I don't think I'm going to tell you.
Crispin:	Can I guess?
Brett:	You can try, but I don't think you'll guess this one.
Crispin:	Did you go to Mama Ayisha's? Is it a banana nut loaf?
Brett:	Naw, you make much better bread than any store, even Ayisha's.
Crispin:	Oh, oh—clue. He gave me a clue. It's something I don't make. The only thing I don't make for us is drugs. What did you get? Come on, Brett, tell me. Is it Sensemia?
Brett:	No, pot-head. Okay, I'll give you a hint.
Crispin:	Okay.
Brett:	In ancient Greece wine was considered to be the nectar of the gods, right?
Crispin:	Yes.
Brett:	And, Matza is synonymous with exodus, right?
Crispin:	Bad clue, not really the same.
Brett:	Hold on. What do you think of when you hear "bread and wine", huh?
Crispin:	Jesus.
Brett:	What part of Jesus?
Crispin:	Body and blood… You brought me what? What Brett? What have you done?
Brett:	I have brought you the truly ultimate in transubstantiation. This beats bread and wine by a millennium. Bread and wine are just symbols. This will bring you the immanent God, the God within. The trinity is dead.
Crispin:	Brett, you jerk. That's a sugar cube. You didn't bring me anything. You just made it up.
Brett:	That's not just any little cube of refined white sugar. Each of these little babies contains $1/350^{th}$ of a gram of D-Lysergic Acid Diethylamide Tartrate. LSD.
Crispin:	Acid? As in Leary? You did it?
Brett:	*(Singing a jingle)* Acid, a little tab'll do ya', you'll love to run your brainwaves through the air. Hotch-cha-cha.

Crispin:	Where did you get it?
Brett:	Boosy and Chris. Come on, let's eat. I'm dyin' to turn ya on t' this stuff. God! Making love is going to be outrageous.
Crispin:	How do you know I'll like it?
Brett:	You'll like it. Trust me.
Crispin:	How do you know? Leary lost his job at Harvard over it.
Brett:	That was because of Teddy Kennedy.
Crispin:	I think the LSD was the issue.
Brett:	Forget Leary. You love Wordsworth, you'll love this.
Crispin:	What?
Brett:	An LSD high is like being inside Wordsworth, you'll see. It's like dropping an H-bomb on just the left side of the brain; you lose all judgement – all distance – all time. You just are, there is only you and whatever is in front of you and you see it like God sees it. Everything has consciousness. Everything has intelligence. You realize that when God contemplates love, it manifests. He manifests mankind. God isn't outside us, Crispin, there's an inner space; God is us. Each of us. It's so high you can't imagine.
Crispin:	So all I have to do is become what? An inner space voyager and I'll find God? This means that Buck Rogers was wrong? God's not out there living on a star waiting for us to find him?
Brett:	No, not exactly. God is the universe and we are God. I understood it all in an instant as soon as the hallucinations stopped.
Crispin:	Why do I feel that you are Israfel come to announce the end of the world?
Brett:	Because the world as we know it is just an illusion, Crispin. Forget dinner. We don't need dinner. Just drop the acid, you'll see. You'll feel it. The rebirth of your spirit.
Crispin:	You're high right now, aren't you?
Brett:	This stuff's awesome.
Crispin:	Alright, but you'll have to explain it to my mother if I dematerialize or something. I heard some guy ate a live kitten while he was high on this stuff.
Brett:	Oooo. Gross!
Crispin:	What if we revert to cannibalism?
Brett:	I wish you hadn't said that.
Crispin:	What?
Brett:	The cat thing. It's bumming me out.
Crispin:	Sorry.

Brett:	You gotta be careful what you say with this shit. 'Cause it'll kinda be real if you say it.
Crispin:	Are you okay?
Brett:	Yeah. You ready?
Crispin:	There's nothin' you need to tell me first.
Brett:	Didn't I just tell you? *(She puts the sugar cube in her mouth.)* Just be. Bee in the moment little bumble bee.
Crispin:	Now I am a bumble bee?
Brett:	You is what you is. You is metaphysical.
Crispin:	And you are metaphysically absurd, my little hobgoblin.

Missing Persons

Premise: **He** I am a man, she is a woman; we have a relationship, we used to be lovers. We are in my office. I haven't seen her since she married Jim.

                    She I am a woman, he is a man; we have a relationship, we used to be lovers. We are in his office. I haven't seen him since I married Jim. Jim is dead.

Tom: Joanna.

Joanna: Hello Tom. It's been a long time. You're looking very prosperous. Your offices are very impressive.

Tom: I've been lucky. In business. Why have you come to the city? And why have you come here of all places? I'm not objecting, just curious. Your message sounded…

Joanna: What?

Tom: I don't know…formal.

Joanna: I need your help, Tom. I'm sure you heard that Jim died this winter.

Tom: Yes, I did. I'm sorry.

Joanna: I've decided to sell the business. The farm, the mill, everything.

Tom: That's risky so soon after his death. People will think you're in trouble. They'll try to take advantage of you. Can't you wait a year?

Joanna: No. I couldn't do that. I've made up my mind. I've come to you because I don't want the whole world to know. I want you to find me a good buyer and I'll come to favorable terms. I don't want a lot of talk and I don't want a lot of people coming around. I couldn't bear it.

Tom: Why me? I would have thought you'd pick anyone but me.

Joanna:	You know me better than anyone. I trust you.
Tom:	I don't wish to be disrespectful of your situation, but you sure have a funny way of showing it.
Joanna:	When I fell in love with Jim, I didn't stop loving you. I couldn't marry you both. He made a good life for me.
Tom:	I know that. People tried to tell me that you married him because he was established. I guess they thought that would make me feel better. It didn't. It didn't because I knew he really loved you and I knew all the reasons why.
Joanna:	That's kind of you to say.
Tom:	That's me. Kind to a fault.
Joanna:	Tom…

Tom:	I'm sorry you lost him, Joanna. I truly am.
Joanna:	He had worked so hard to build up the mill and the business. It was almost as if he had to do it to prove himself worthy. I think that's why he hadn't married when he was younger. He was so completely at home there. He knew every beam and joint of the buildings, every nut and bolt of the machinery. He was like a kid who had built this gigantic toy that actually worked and did something useful.
Tom:	You don't have to explain…
Joanna:	I want you to understand why it has to be quick and quiet. That place is Jim. It's him and I can't bear it. I can't bear being there or the thought of selling it all.
Tom:	I have tried for a long time to work up a good strong hate for you. Anything to get you out of my system and now, here you are…a widow much too soon. And I am ashamed of the things I'm feeling.
Joanna:	This was a mistake. Tom, I'm sorry.
Tom:	And pleased, I might add.
Joanna:	What?
Tom:	As hard as I tried, I couldn't find one good excuse to hate you. I'm just realizing why.
Joanna:	Tell me this wasn't a monumental mistake.
Tom:	No. It isn't. It's very right. In some cosmic, karmic way, which defies description, I am very glad you came to me. I've imagined you walking through that door so many times I thought I'd go mad. I wanted you to tell me you'd made a terrible mistake and that it was me you really loved. I never pictured you a widow and I never pictured you telling me how much you truly love Jim and all the good reasons why. But here you are doing both.
Joanna:	Am I being selfish?
Tom:	Yes.
Joanna:	I never knew I'd have to make such choices in my life.
Tom:	You've made the right ones. Then and now. No recriminations. Not now, not ever.
Joanna:	Will you help me, Tom?
Tom:	Yes, Mrs. Pintero, I will.

The Evening News

Premise: **He**   I am a man, she is a woman; we work together. We are on the set of our news program. There has been a school bus accident. We are on the air.

                      She   I am a woman, he is a man; we work together. We are on the set of our news program. There has been a school bus accident. We are on the air.

Georgia: This evening's news is brought to you by…John, why don't you tell our viewers who our sponsors are.

John: The news is brought to you by Baxter and Gumble, makers of fine home healthcare products for over seventy-five years.

Georgia: Are we off? John, I'm sorry. I went blank.

John: It's okay.

Georgia: It's not okay. I shouldn't have blown such a simple thing. Hey! Obie, can you cut the lights a little, I'm going blind up here.

John: You have bad fish for lunch?

Georgia: I feel like a robot. Words come out of my mouth but they have no meaning to me. Marge, how much time before we're back on?

John: Forty five. It's displayed on your monitor. You better get a hold of yourself.

Georgia: I can't look. Is there film on it?

John: Yes, in fact Barry's still on the scene. I think they've got the school bus out of the gulch now. We're gonna cut to him.

Georgia: Deaths?

John: Yeah, lots, it's all there on your poop sheet.

Georgia: Yes, of course it is. John, I can't go on and report about a busload of dead kids. How much time have we got?

John: We're at fifteen.

Georgia:	Marge, put on another commercial… John, how can they expect me to do this? How many mothers and father…
John:	We're going on.
Georgia:	Damn.
John:	Georgia, listen to me, you've done this kind of thing hundreds of times. You can do it…
Georgia:	That's just it, I've done it so much I feel like I don't feel anything anymore. Children aren't the Dow Jones Average. I swear to God, John. I don't know what's going to come out of my mouth.
John:	We're out of time.
Georgia:	What's first? No, not the school bus!
John:	Just read your copy. Don't think about it. Think of your career.
Georgia:	Fuck my career. *(To the camera.)* There was tragedy late this afternoon on the Ventura Freeway when an L.A. Unified bus went out of control and crashed through two sets of guard rails to a fiery end at the bottom of a roadside gulch. First reports claimed that all eighty-seven children and the bus driver were killed. But later reports seem to disagree. KRAK's Barry Coldar is at the scene…
	Are we off? Turn off my monitor. Obie, Obie turn of my monitor. I can't watch.
John:	You're committing professional suicide, you know that, don't you?
Georgia:	All I know is that there are eighty-seven mothers and fathers out there whose lives will never be the same. Their children have just become highway statistics and they never got a chance to grow up.
John:	We can talk about it later. I'll buy you a drink. The boys upstairs don't pay us for our reactions. We're reporters.
Georgia:	We're human. We report what happens to human beings.
John:	Barry's wrapping up. You're on.
Georgia:	That's the scene on the Ventura Freeway, where a school bus accident occurred late this afternoon. Victim's names are being withheld until families are notified. Now, a look at today's political scene with John Rutledge. John.
John:	Hearings continued today in the investigation into the slaughter of hundreds of Palestinians, including many women and children. At this point there is still no conclusive evidence to say who is to blame. We'll have a report from foreign correspondent Josh Freeman, after a word from our sponsor.

The Last Shall Be First

Premise: **He** I am a man, she is a woman; we have a relationship, she's my wife. We are in our home. It's late at night. We are having a baby.

She I am a woman, he is a man; we have a relationship, he is my husband. We're in our home. I found out today that I am pregnant.

Jack: Joni? You alright?

Joni: I couldn't sleep.

Jack: Pretty exciting, huh?

Joni: Uh-huh.

Jack: Do you feel different? I mean, now that you know for sure? Can I get you something? Milk? Tea? A Pickle?

Joni: No. Thanks. Jack, I need to tell you something.

Jack: What?

Joni: Oh man. I don't know exactly…

Jack: This is my baby right?

Joni: Jesus. Of course it is. I should have told you this a long time ago.

Jack: Okay. Shoot.

(Joni pauses.)

Jack: Come on Joni.

Joni: My father didn't leave home when I was an infant like I told you.

Jack: You knew him?

Joni: Know him. Sort of.

Jack: Where is he?

Joni: He's a successful businessman. Right here in town.

Jack: You see him?

Joni: No, not since I was twelve.

Jack: Why did you lie to me?

Joni: It's how we dealt with it. It was easier if I treated it as though he had actually left..

Jack: What are you talking about?

Joni: I thought it was all behind me, but when Dr. Howe told me I was pregnant today I got scared.

Jack: Of what? What's this all about?

Joni: My mother kicked my father out because she found him in bed with me. It wasn't the first time.

Jack: He molested you?

Joni: He had sex with me, Jack. Something's wrong, Jack. All day I've been trying to be happy, but I'm so scared. I haven't felt this way since back then, but the instant I knew I had a child growing inside of me I felt bad again, like it's wrong. I lied to you. Something's going to be wrong with it, I know.

Jack: You know no such thing. You just held all this in too long. It's gotten distorted.

Joni: The child has my father's genes, just like I do. I should have died before my mother found out. I can't have this baby, Jack.

Jack: We are gonna have this baby, Joni. It's ours. It's what we want.

Joni: I know you want it, Jack.

Jack: Who is your father?

Joni: No.

Jack: What's his name?

Joni: I can't tell you. He still supports my mother.

Jack: Jesus Christ!

Joni: She didn't want people to find out. She didn't want him in jail. She needed him to support us.

Jack: You've lived with this so your mother could blackmail your father?

Joni: She thought it was the best way to deal with it. I was scared. I didn't know what to do.

Jack: They should both be in jail.

Joni: She thought she was protecting me.

Jack: She was holding you hostage.

Joni: I don't know if I can do this, Jack.

Jack: You've got me now. We can make it right.

Joni;   I think it's too late for that.

Jack: Tell me who your father is.

Joni:	I can't.
Jack:	This isn't just you and your parents now. This is my baby too. This is my life.
Joni:	You see? You see how complicated it is? If we have a baby it changes everything.
Jack:	Oh my God. Oh my God. Okay, honey look. We'll find out what to do. But, we can do this…together.
Joni:	Don't, don't…don't say anything to Mom.
Jack:	Your mother? Don't you see that what she has done is as wrong as what your father did?
Joni:	She needed to take care of me.
Jack:	She wanted to make your father pay and she used you for ransom.
Joni:	Yes.
Jack:	We'll take it slow. You don't have to tell me now. Okay?
Joni:	Okay.
Jack:	I love you.
Joni:	I know. I'm sorry.
Jack:	You have nothing to apologize for.
Joni:	I should have told you.
Jack:	Perhaps. Let's not look backward now. What we need to do is look ahead.

To The Moon and Back

Premise: **He** I am a man, she is a woman; we are meeting for the first time. We are at a party.

She I am a woman, he is a man; we are meeting for the first time. We are at a party.

He: Is this seat taken?

She: No.

He: Okay if I join you?

She: Guess so.

He: Life is funny, don't you think?

She: It's not what I'm thinking at the moment.

He: I guess what I really mean is that people are funny, don't you think?

She: Yeah, well. Smoke gets in your eyes.

He: Maybe I should move, do you think?

She: You don't have to move on my account.

He: Oh.

She: What is it about people you find to be funny?

He: How we behave. Events such as these. It's an event. A social event. Supposed to be fun. None of us is having fun. We're tense. We're alienated, but the band keeps playing and no matter what song they play, I hear the same words. "Put on a happy face". I'm too intense, aren't I?

She: Too intense for what?

He: Now there's a question. It's my card. My advance man. My vanguard. It's the thing that walks in front of me, knocking people out of the way before I get a chance to know them. Before they get a chance to know me.

She:	What are you talking about?
He:	My neurotic intensity. I think I make people uncomfortable. I'm terrified of a moment of silence.
She:	What's to fear in the silence?
He:	Loneliness. My loneliness. My heart beating by itself, filling my ears with its earnest thumping. Good God, what am I saying? What's your name?
She:	I could tell you my name, but something tells me it would change the conversation.
He:	That's intense. I mean it's an intense thought. Actually, it has intense implications. Are you saying this conversation is okay with you?
She:	So far so good.
He:	Wow.
She:	Yeah, wow.
He:	You don't say a lot, but when you do it's got a punch. In a good way, a good punch. Punch good, kemo sabe.
She:	Why don't you ask your advance man to take five? See what happens.
He:	Are you serious? Yes, I can see you are. Bye pal, take five. Take ten. In fact, I'll call ya when I need ya. Atta-boy, bye-bye. There. Done. We're all alone. Say something.
She:	I've got an island in the Pacific. Just kidding.
He:	Too bad.
She:	Wouldn't it be a kick to just rewrite the rules? To just say what's true in the moment? I feel the tug of collective thought. I feel myself tugging to get away from it. It's like a huge river rushing past with such a force it pulls you in before you realize it. The roar of it blocks out your own thoughts.
He:	What thoughts are you having right now?
She:	I'm thinking, "This guy's got a soul. He's trying the best he can. He wants his soul to shine in the world just like I want mine to. Why should it be so difficult?"
He:	Boy, when you think, you take it seriously.
She:	Not always. I can be light. Really.
He:	I'm sure.
She:	There is something in this moment, this rare opportunity to meet each other on undiscovered soil, outside the ruts from other peoples wheels. Every once in a vast time span two people come together without baggage, without expectation, without prejudice and they can look at each other and see each other clearly, cleanly.

As God sees them. This is one of those moments if we treat it so. It feels sacred, deeply silent, swollen with life.

He: I feel as though you are speaking to me from a place deep inside the earth.

She: Yes?

He: The womb of all possibility.

She: Go on.

He: As if you are calling up the wisdom of all time to hold us in this moment. As if creation itself was lending us eyes to see with.

She: I don't think I'm doing it by myself.

He: It feels like it's happening through you, or because of you.

She: The part of me, which can't be named…the part of you, which can't be named.

He: Is it possible that there is a place… no, not a place. A what? A state in which we exist as a joint creation of each other? I don't talk like this.

She: You do right now. And very well, I might add.

He: Isn't it marvelous?

She: Yes.

He: Where do we go from here?

She: To the moon and back.

He: Can we?

She: Can't we?

He: I rather like this nameless state.

Female/Female
Scenes

Aloha

Premise: **Nancy** I am a woman, she is a woman; we are meeting for the first time. We are in a hotel in Hawaii.

Patsy I am a woman, she is a woman; we are meeting for the first time. We are in a hotel in Hawaii.

Nancy: Gosh this is pretty. Did you just check in?

Patsy: Yeah.

Nancy: I thought so. In fact, I think we were on the same flight. Northwest from L.A.?

Patsy: Yeah.

Nancy: See. I knew it. Is this your first time in Hawaii?

Patsy: Yeah.

Nancy: Mine too. I'm so excited. You don't feel like talking, do you?

Patsy: Just trying to get used to being here.

Nancy: Oh, I don't want to get used to it. I don't want this feeling to stop.

Patsy: It's nice that you feel that way.

Nancy: I hear they serve drinks everywhere here. Is it too early to drink?

Patsy: I've been reading this little guide to the hotel. It says if you just sit still for a moment a waiter will pop up out of nowhere to take your order. Pretty strange, huh?

Nancy: Now that's something I might get used to.

Patsy: What's the occasion? How come you're here.

Nancy: Job burn-out. I'm the charge nurse in the ICU at Cedars-Sinai. It can get pretty intense. No pun intended. Most of our patients are heart patients. If one of them goes into cardiac arrest while I'm on duty I'm the one in charge of giving orders. There are very specific procedures you have to go through and you have to be totally familiar with the patient's history 'cause too much epinephrine, even in the initial stages of an attack, can kill the patient. Also when you're ventilating them you have to be careful not to burst their lungs. It can be very stressful. Most of our patients die. After awhile it gets pretty depressing. So I'm here in Hawaii getting a little attitude adjustment. How about you?

Patsy: I guess you might say I'm experiencing the same thing. Job burn-out. Actually, my mother died and left me a little money so I thought I might as well treat myself nice. I've given up on the white knight. Mom died waiting for hers to arrive.

Nancy: I'm sorry. If you'd like to be alone I'll understand.

Patsy: No. Really, it's alright. I wasn't that close to her. We were probably too much alike to ever get along, I guess.

Nancy: What kind of work do you do?

Patsy: I'm a model.

Nancy: I hear that's a nerve-wracking business. You based in L.A. or New York?

Patsy: I'm not a model.

Nancy: Oh.

Patsy: I'm an escort. A call girl.

Nancy: Okay.

Patsy: Shocked?

Nancy: A little, but not as much as you'd think. Working in a hospital, surprises are what you expect. I'm not judging you if that's what you think. So...thinking about changing things?

Patsy: I'd love to. I'm real tired of men and stupid little Mr. Wiggly. They all come along thinking theirs is the greatest. They think they're gonna make a difference in your life. They're all the same; they just don't want to...I'm sorry. Didn't mean to go off.

Nancy: Let 'er rip, honey – you're on vacation.

Patsy: The truth is, a penis is about the ugliest thing God ever created.

Nancy: Almost, anyway. I'll never forget the first cadaver I ever worked on. My lab partner and I used to joke that he'd died of fright lookin' in the mirror. He probably looked a little better when he was alive. But not much. I guess in your life and mine they all start to look alike after awhile.

Patsy: Pretty much. There have been a few exceptions though.

Nancy: Thank God for that, huh? Hey, I am dying to get my feet in that Hawaiian surf. How about a walk?

Patsy: Sounds good to me. What's your name?

Nancy: Nancy. What's yours?

Patsy: Patsy. If you changed jobs what'd you do?

Nancy: I'd like to run a flower shop. I always thought that would be a very pleasant way to live. How about you?

Patsy: I'd like to be an artist. I'd come by your shop and paint pictures of you and your flowers.

Nancy: I could sell your paintings in my shop.

Patsy: God, it would be nice.

Nancy: People do, you know.

Patsy: What?

Nancy: Change their lives.

Patsy: On the outside maybe.

Nancy: You don't think you change inside?

Patsy: I can't imagine that that could really happen.

Nancy: I think it does all the time. I think we're constantly changing on the inside. We grow; we get older, different things start to matter 'cause we've changed on the inside.

Patsy: Maybe.

Nancy: The trouble comes if we don't make changes on the outside to go with the changes that are already happening in the inside.

Patsy: You learn that in nursing school?

Nancy: Nursing school isn't that deep. I learned it in the school of life – same as you.

Patsy: Same as me. I wouldn't know where to begin.

Nancy: A walk on the beach in Hawaii is about as good a place as any.

Patsy: I hear ya.

Dear Yo-Ho

Premise: **Colleen** I am a woman, she is a woman; we have a relationship, we are friends. We are at my house.

Lola I am a woman, she is a woman; we have a relationship, we are friends. We are at her house. I am pregnant.

Colleen: Francis is finally moving out.

Lola: I'll believe it when the last pile of dirty clothes is gone.

Colleen: I think I finally realize what it is about him you found so distasteful.

Lola: Did he ever learn to close doors or turn out the lights?

Colleen: I really can't bear to talk about it. It wasn't just the doors and the lights. He never did any housework and always drank Larry's beer. Larry's much too nice to him. I don't want to talk about it.

Lola: Okay.

Colleen: I knew he'd really gone too far when he showed up at my office in a very brief running costume and said he wanted to talk. Do you know he'd been leaving his keys under the snapdragons in the front garden for all the world to see? He didn't like to carry keys when he ran. We live in the city, for Christ's sake. He didn't mind wearing his Walkman, I noticed. I just can't discuss this anymore. Tell me about Kirk.

Lola: We were supposed to meet after work, but he called at lunchtime. Ray-Ray broke his pelvis and refused medical attention. Some phobia about hospitals. Ricky's mother died so Kirk had to...

Colleen: Who is Ricky?

Lola: Ray-Ray's porno-star boyfriend. His mother died so Kirk had to help Ray get put together for the funeral. Kirk's still only working part-time so all his friends rely on him a lot.

Colleen: Take advantage of him, you mean. Want a bourbon and soda?

Lola: No thanks. Got any wine?

Colleen: I hope so. If we don't it's because Francis drank it all. That little twit. You know, I wouldn't have minded his showing up at my office half-naked except he came in yelling at me because he thought I'd taken his keys out of the garden to teach him a lesson. I was not in a good mood because we had not gotten much sleep the night before.

Lola: What happened?

Colleen: Two o'clock in the morning, we hear women's voices outside, then, bam bam on the door. Larry looked out the window and there are two hookers on our front porch calling for Francis. Larry hollered upstairs to Francis, who was on his way downstairs with yet another hooker. I was in the hall by then, and said, "What's going on here?" He seemed annoyed at the question.

Lola: Colleen. Just because he's your brother doesn't mean you have to put up with all that.

Colleen: I know. Larry gave him three days to get out. On the third day he came into the kitchen after dinner and told us he hadn't been able to find a new room and asked to stay 'til the end of the month. Larry was a gentleman and said, "Yes", of course. I said nothing. I was doing the dishes, crashing them around and splashing water all over the floor. He seemed to sense my displeasure and asked, "What are you thinking?"… "Nothing good" was all I said. Lola, he's my brother. I want to love him, but I swear to God, Mom and Dad didn't leave me much to work with.

Lola: I should come around more often. This place is better than *General Hospital*.

Colleen: We'll see if we make it to the end of the month. Please tell me something new about you.

Lola: I'm thinking about marrying Kirk, but I'm not sure. I'm pregnant you see, and I think it's Kirk's baby…

Colleen: Whoa!

Colleen: Lola?

Lola: Yes?

Colleen: You're pregnant?

Lola: Pretty cool, huh?

Colleen: Kirk's?

Lola: Mostly positive.

Colleen: That's not an answer.

Lola: Yes it is.

Colleen: An answer would be yes…

Lola: It's the best I can do.

Colleen: …or, no.

Lola: That's not the point.

Colleen: What is the point?

Lola: The point is that Kirk and
            Joe used to be lovers...   Colleen: Your Joe?
            Yeah, and since Joe and I
            used to be lovers too, it would
            be very disconcerting to sit
            down at Christmas dinner
            with both of them.

Colleen: Jesus Christ, Lola. What are you talking about? Why would you
            have to be at Christmas dinner with both of them?

Lola: Because Joe asked Kirk's sister, Jeanie, to marry him last week,
            didn't I tell you? He'd be my brother-in-law. I don't think Jeanie
            knows about me and Joe or about Joe and Kirk.

Colleen: Now that's a progressive family.

Lola: Should I do it?

Colleen: You lost me.

Lola: Marry Kirk?

Colleen: You are not seriously asking me what you should do?

Lola: Yes.

Colleen: If anyone could pull this off it's you. Do you love him?

Lola: I think he's different.

Colleen: Do you like him?

Lola: Of course I like him.

Colleen: Well, like is a good thing. Hell, maybe like lasts longer than love.

Lola: I think he'd be a good father.

Colleen: That's important.

Lola: I'm gonna do it.

Colleen: Great.

Lola: Matron of Honor?

Colleen: Who, me?

Lola: Yes.

Colleen: I wouldn't miss being a part of this. I'm there.

Lola: Good God, I'm really doing this!

Miss Liberty

Premise: **Carole Ann**   I am a woman, she is a woman; we have a relationship, she is my mother. We are in our home. I am leaving today to join the convent.

Margaret   I am a woman, she is a woman; we have a relationship, she is my daughter. We are in our home. She is leaving today to become a nun.

Carole Ann: There, I think I'm finally all packed. Will you change your mind and come to the station with me and Daddy?

Margaret: No.

Carole Ann: Why are you being this way?

Margaret: You are just trying to make me emotional and it won't work. If you want to go and waste your life, that's your business, but don't expect me to stand by and cheer you on.

Carole Ann: I'm not wasting my life. I can't believe you see it that way. You are the one who taught me to respect nuns. You say they are a sacred breed of women.

Margaret: Honey, women become nuns when they don't have any other alternative. You have alternatives. We've given you the best education money can buy, we've worked hard to give you every advantage. I can't believe you're going to throw it all away.

Carole Ann: I am not throwing anything away. This is a chance for me to reach out to the world. To be part of a larger world than Mystic, Connecticut; to do something that has an impact.

Margaret: You want to see the world, join the Navy. At least there you'd meet a man.

Carole Ann: And then what? Get married, move to the suburbs, have kids and be a laundress and a baby-sitter for the next twenty years? No thanks.

Margaret: Is that how you see me? As a laundress and a baby-sitter? Is that all?

Carole Ann: No Mom, of course not.

Margaret: Nice to know you've considered me your servant all these years.

Carole Ann: For goodness sake, no, Mother.

Margaret: Do you think it was easy? I managed a household, for God's sake. Five people's lives, day in, day out.

Carole Ann: I'm not putting you down. It's just not for me.

Margaret: You are so ungrateful. You don't realize what we've done for you.

Carole Ann: I am not ungrateful, just the opposite…

Margaret: You pass judgment on me. Is that not ungrateful?

Carole Ann: Not you – it's the job description. Not you – you're a wonderful mother.

Margaret: Oh please, don't be condescending.

Carole Ann: I can't win with you.

Margaret: What do you know about mothering? You don't even want to be a mother. You're just a selfish little brat.

Carole Ann: Let's not get into name-calling. Dad's waiting. I'd better go.

Margaret: What went wrong? We were so careful raising you.

Carole Ann: Nothing went wrong, Mother. I've chosen to be a missionary, not a hooker.

Margaret: Your father and I didn't spend forty thousand dollars on your bachelor's degree so you could go die of malaria in some jungle in Central America.

Carole Ann: Don't include Daddy in this. He doesn't have a problem with my choice.

Margaret: Your father never had good sense. He spoils you kids. Anything you want…presto. He's too easy on you, I'll tell you that.

Carole Ann: Stop it. Stop blaming everyone for the things you can't understand.

Margaret: You think you know so much more than me? You don't know anything about life—about the real world. You're just a kid.

Carole Ann: Mom, why can't you just say you're going miss me? Why all this drama?

Margaret: No – you are not going to make me all emotional.

Carole Ann: Oh really?

Margaret: Don't be sarcastic.

Carole Ann: Come on, Mom. What is this, if you're not all emotional?

Margaret: It's my last chance to talk you out of a very bad decision.

Carole Ann: You waited 'til now? You give me the silent treatment for three weeks and now you want to talk about it?

Margaret: Well, if you're going to be all huffy, never mind.

Carole Ann: I'm not huffy, I'm late.

Margaret: Then go. Don't be late.

Carole Ann: You are a piece of work.

Margaret: Go.

Carole Ann: Come with us.

Margaret: No.

Carole Ann: Alright. Well, bye then.

(Carole Ann begins to leave.)

Margaret: Be careful.

Carole Ann: *(Turns back.)* What?

Margaret: In the jungle. Be careful.

Carole Ann: I will. I promise.

(They hug.)

Margaret: I'll be praying for you.

Carole Ann: Bye.

Rainfall

Premise: **Sue** I am a woman, she is a woman; we have a relationship, she is my sister. We are in her house.

                           Kay I am a woman, she is a woman; we have a relationship, she is my sister. We are in my house.

Sue: Could you turn off the radio? I want to hear the rain.

Kay: Why not, rain's fun.

Sue: It's soothing.

Kay: Fine.

Sue: I shouldn't be here, should I?

Kay: You being here isn't the problem.

Sue: What is?

Kay: Your attitude is the problem.

Sue: What is my attitude? Just exactly how do you see it?

Kay: It's like water dripping. It's just there, this background irritation. I don't know. Sue, why can't you live and let live?

Sue: I'm trying, Kay. The best I can. I'm really trying. I ask God every day to guide me through. I don't want to fight with Mom and Dad, but something's there. You're right, it's like water dripping. Dad looks at me and I want to kill him. I don't know why. But every time he looks at me it's like he's saying, "Don't".

Kay: Don't what?

Sue: I don't know. "Don't ask any questions. Don't look for the truth."

Kay: Why come back here if you're feeling this way?

Sue: I want answers, Kay. Where else can I get them?

Kay: Answers to what? What are you looking for?

Sue: Why my life went haywire. Why I can't remember half my childhood. You were there. You could help me.

Kay:	Susan, most of us forget the majority of our childhood. Why remember? Digging in the dirt, swinging on a swing, feeling awkward, hating our teachers. What's the point of remembering that?
Sue:	Don't be obtuse. You know that's not what I'm talking about.
Kay:	Okay, what are you talking about?
Sue:	How we were nurtured.
Kay:	What about it?
Sue:	I'm not very good at it and I'm wondering why.
Kay:	Good at nurturing?
Sue:	Yeah.
Kay:	Why do you think you're not good at it?
Sue:	Come on, Kay. Look at me. I mean, look at my life. Everyone takes this apparently kind attitude that Sue's still finding herself, but no one can actually say, "Sue's lost".
Kay:	Oh, honey. Is that how you're feeling? Are you feeling lost?
Sue:	Yes. Is that really such a surprise to you?
Kay:	Half and half. I have always assumed that you live the way you live because you want it that way.
Sue:	What do you mean, the way I live?
Kay:	I'm not judging you.
Sue:	That's not what I'm thinking. Tell me, how would you describe the way I live?
Kay:	Independently.
Sue:	Alone.
Kay:	Oh.
Sue:	I'm not criticizing you. I'm just pointing out how the family can't really see me the way I am. Which, I admit, is no picnic.
Kay:	We love you, honey.
Sue:	Do you? Do you even know me? How can you love me if you don't even know me?
Kay:	You're my sister.
Sue:	I like *War and Peace* because it's a good book. That doesn't mean I could sit in a room with Tolstoy for more than five minutes 'cause I don't really know him. He might be very hard to deal with.
Kay:	I hear that he was.
Sue:	What?
Kay:	Hard to deal with.
Sue:	Stick to the subject.

Kay:	Which is?
Sue:	Saying you love me because I'm your sister isn't the same as saying you like me because of who I am.
Kay:	Yes it is. I've known you my whole life. I've watched you grow. I mean... we grew together, for God's sake. I do know you.
Sue:	That's funny.
Kay:	I don't think it's funny.
Sue:	No you wouldn't. It's funny that you can say with such conviction that you know me. Because I don't. Know me. All I know is this fear that I'm constantly managing. But that's not me. It can't be me.
Kay:	Of course it isn't.
Sue:	I mean, why am I me and you, you? We were made by the same parents. I mean, why aren't I you? I could be you. I could have a family and a nice home. If I were you. Why did it happen that I'm me and you're you?
Kay:	If any of us could answer that, we'd get the Nobel Prize for something, I'm sure.
Sue:	You're so good at this.
Kay:	What?
Sue:	Being alternately glib, then sincere. Sincere, and then glib. As if we were actually having a normal conversation.
Kay:	What's not normal?
Sue:	Oh, come on, Kay. Even I know this is a dark, bleak conversation. I know I'm testing you. Seeing how close I can get you to come.
Kay:	To what, honey?
Sue:	The edge. Isn't that odd? It really feels like an edge. Like a cliff above an endless, dark ravine. And even though I know I'm doing it, I can't stop myself.
Kay:	Sue. That's just your depression talking.
Sue:	I'm tiptoeing along a narrowing edge. And here you are trotting along with me. Dutiful daughter that you are.
Kay:	I'm your sister. It's what sisters are sometimes called upon to do.
Sue:	I was assigned to you. I became your burden.
Kay:	You are not a burden.
Sue:	Your voice and your manner don't reflect the real agony of the place we're in right now. Don't you want to scream, Kay? Don't you want to shake me and yell, "Snap out if it Sue!" because I would sincerely like to do that myself. I'm just not up to it.
Kay:	Don't you have some meds that help you with this?

Sue:	The meds aren't working.
Kay:	Oh, honey. I do love you. It breaks my heart to see you this way. But I have to say I don't know what to do.
Sue:	You can't imagine how completely alone in the world I feel.
Kay:	I will help you. I will find out how to help you. Or, so help me, I'll die trying.
Sue:	Oh, don't do that. Someone might think this disease is catching.
Kay:	You know, we all feel alone and lonely sometimes. Even with a husband and kids driving me crazy, I sometimes feel alone and misunderstood.
Sue:	Thank you for saying that. Even if it's not true.
Kay:	It's true, believe me. None of us can escape our own skin.
Sue:	Now, that is the truth, sister. That is God's honest truth. Listen to that rain. Just coming down and coming down.
Kay:	Makes the air fresh, doesn't it?
Sue:	Um hmm.
Kay:	It is soothing.
Sue:	Told you.

The Rug

Premise:
Margot I am a woman, she is a woman; we have a relationship, she is my decorator. We are in my apartment.

Bobbie I am a woman, she is a woman; we have a relationship, she is my client. We are in her apartment.

Margot: Bobbie? Bobbie darling, are you here? I saw the...MY GOD! What is that?

Bobbie: "Roses of Life", *Max Canby*. Isn't it fantastic?

Margot: Did I buy it?

Bobbie: Yep. And when Sylvia Shaft finds out, she'll die. Just flat out die.

Margot: Are you sure it's right for the room? I mean, does it go with the *John Phillipe* style? What kind of rugs did *John Phillipe* have?

Bobbie: The theme is *Louis Phillipe*. Please try to remember. It's Louis, not John.

Margot: Theme, Style, John, Louis, Phillip; my head is swimming. I'd pictured something a little more Cape Coddish. Do you really think it goes?

Bobbie: Sweetheart, I don't think anything. I know. This is the coup of the season. I nearly fainted when I saw it at Fierce and Frock.

Margot: This room is getting harder and harder to relax in. What if I just want to read a book? You know, just curl up on the couch.

Bobbie: You read in the bedroom. That's why I selected "Violet Infusion" in brushed cotton. It's perfect for reading.

Margot: Whose apartment is this? I like to read by the fire.

Bobbie: Margot, trust me. This living room, this whole apartment is going to be the talk of the town. Just wait and see.

Margot: I can imagine.

Bobbie:	I've made a list of my friends for you to invite to the christening party. You'll be sure to get into one of the major mags before Christmas. Here. Now put it somewhere safe, those names are gold.
Margot:	Thelma Thacker? Bo Bellieu? Bobbie, these people are famous. I can't invite them to my party. I haven't even said I was giving a party.
Bobbie:	Of course you are, silly. Broadway's newest darling can't redecorate her new co-op and not give a party. That would be so rude. Besides, when you have your invitations printed, you announce that your home has been recently redressed by Bobbie Brattavitch. They'll come.
Margot:	Seems a bit nouveau to me. Bobbie, I don't mean to be unappreciative. This is still so new to me. I have been splitting corned beef sandwiches with Myrna at the Stage Door most of my adult life and now…now it's all different. I'm doing "luncheon at The Lincoln Center", my second show is a hit, I've got a co-op on 76th street, and…
Bobbie:	And you've got me to decorate for you. Relax, Margot.
Margot:	Relax? Bobbie. Every time I come home there's a new little treasure that cost more than my parents' house in Scranton. None of this feels real. I feel out of control.
Bobbie:	That's the best part. We're still under budget.
Margot:	Oh, that's good. I'll be able to afford one good meal before I'm arrested for "consumerato en flagrante".
Bobbie:	Wait a minute Margot. Before you start getting dramatic. These are all fantastic investments. Now, that painting over the fireplace, that's a *Theodore Robinson*. The candlesticks are *Hester Bateman*. These are names Margot, great names. God knows how much they'll appreciate. You'll thank me in your golden years.
Margot:	Bobbie, you're a sweetheart. Really you are. I'll be grateful if I make it to my golden years without becoming a raving lunatic, or, worse yet, a burnt out genius who sits around drooling and speaking gibberish all day and night. You don't think that'll happen to me, do you Bobbie?
Bobbie:	If you really don't like the rug, I'll take it back. I'm sure Mr. Fierce will understand. I'll just take it back, he'll understand. I'm sure he will. It won't be a problem. I'll just take back the *Max Canby* rug and tell Mr. Fierce you didn't like it. Will that make you feel better?
Margot:	I'm sorry, Bobbie. I'd like to like it.
Bobbie:	I hope you know what this is doing to me.
Margot:	It's just a rug.
Bobbie:	Not in my world, honey.

Twilight

Premise: **Kathy** I am a woman, she is a woman; we have a
relationship, she is my mother. We are in her house.
I am helping her pack.

Peggy I am a woman, she is a woman; we have a
relationship, she is my daughter. We are in my house.
I am packing to move.

Kathy: Mom, where are the linens I put out in the hall?

Peggy: I packed them.

Kathy: Oh. In which box?

Peggy: Never you mind.

Kathy: Sure, whatever.

Peggy: I know what you're thinking.

Kathy: Sorry. I just don't feel like I'm being that much help.

Peggy: Yes you are, dear, I couldn't do it without you.

Kathy: Then why do you keep undoing everything I do? It feels like we're
doing everything twice.

Peggy: We wouldn't if you'd ask me first, before you give my things to
Good Will.

Kathy: I thought you wanted to get rid of a lot of it.

Peggy: I do.

Kathy: It doesn't look that way.

Peggy: These things may be old and threadbare, but they're mine.

Kathy: I know they're yours Mom, I do. I thought it would help if I made
a few surgical decisions. You can't hold onto it all. There just isn't
going to be room.

Peggy: I'm not trying to be difficult, honey. I didn't expect this to have
such an effect on me. It's harder than I expected. I'm looking
forward to living closer to you all. I thought that would make

this easier. I'm not a hanger on. Half of these things I haven't even looked at in years. Each one I pull out has a whole memory attached to it. Events appear in my head like it was yesterday. Things your father said. Nothing significant really, I can't believe I'm recalling it all in such detail. I swear to God, it's like he's right here with me. I turned around yesterday in the hall, fully expecting to see him there.

Kathy: I'm alright as long as I can be systematic about this. I don't think I can survive blubbering through this whole house. You have far too many closets.

Peggy: Yes I do, don't I? No one needs this many closets. It's ridiculous. You know, right before Daddy died I was thinking about converting one of the guestrooms into a walk-in. It's probably what killed him.

Kathy: Don't.

Peggy: That's probably what did him in. He thought he'd spend his whole retirement going from flea market to shopping mall. He was awfully patient with me.

Kathy: I always suspected he secretly liked it.

Peggy: Did you?

Kathy: Um-hmm. He came home with a few new sweaters and things as I recall.

Peggy: But I picked them out.

Kathy: Of course you did. That's what he liked. He loved you telling him how good he looked in blue.

Peggy: Or mauve.

Kathy: I'd forgotten about that. He was like a little boy who didn't want to put on his slicker.

Peggy: He was so mad at me. I never understood why he got so mad about that sweater. Usually, if he didn't like something he put it in the back of his drawer and forgot about it. Eventually, I would too. But he was furious about the mauve sweater. I thought it looked good with his skin color.

Kathy: Maybe he was in menopause.

Peggy: I think he was afraid of growing old.

Kathy: Really?

Peggy: Yes.

Kathy: Why?

Peggy: He never actually said anything, for one. And he had an opinion on every subject. But mostly I think it's the way he'd look at Bill as Bill got older. And he always got so quiet when the subject of aging came up. Those were the only discussions he never took part in.

Kathy: I miss him so much Mom. How do you manage?

Peggy: Deep down in your heart, you always know. One of you has to go first. You hope it'll be yourself. Then you don't, because you can't bear the thought of him having to bury you. You start praying that God'll want you both at the same time, but you know. You just know that it's what you've spent your whole life preparing for.

Kathy: Dying?

Peggy: No. Gratitude. My life with you father was so rich and wonderful. Just the right proportion of mystery and revelation. I hope you and Jim are having as wonderful a life as Jack and I did.

Kathy: I think you and Dad were a great model. We're very happy together.

Peggy: Jack always told me that. He'd say, "Peggy, stop worrying, it isn't doing these kids any damn good anyway." He had such faith in you. It never occurred to him that you wouldn't be happy.

Kathy: Me either. I just never expected to lose Dad so young.

Peggy: God has a plan bigger that we can see, and purposes deeper than we can fathom.

Kathy: Let's quit for the day. There's no rush.

Peggy: I was hoping you'd say that. I want to take some fresh flowers out to the cemetery. Want to come?

Kathy: More than anything.

Understanding

Premise: **Jill** I am a woman, she is a woman; we have a
             relationship, she is my friend. We are in her studio.

             Pam I am a woman, she is a woman; we have a
             relationship, she is my friend. We are in my studio.

Jill: This is a beauty. I like what you're doing these days. Sophisticated.

Pam: Très.

Jill: You should take yourself more seriously.

Pam: I do. I'm doing what I love.

Jill: Sorry, that's not what I meant. I mean, sometimes I don't think you
           realize how stunningly evocative your work is.

Pam: Are you bucking for agent?

Jill: Can I ask you a question?

Pam: Of course.

Jill: Where is your mind when you're working on your pottery? What
           kinds of things do you think about?

Pam: I think about the pottery.

Jill: What else? Your mind must wander some?

Pam: Inquiring minds want to know? Are you looking for something
           Freudian in this? If you say yes, there's a good possibility I won't
           be your friend anymore.

Jill: Then we're in luck, 'cause I'm not talking Freud.

Pam: Good.

Jill: Not exactly.

Pam: Not good. Jill, I don't want to analyze my work. It'll fuck me up.
           Make me self-conscious. So get it. I'm dead serious. If you're
           about to do that, don't.

Jill: Okay, okay. I hear ya. Indulge me for a moment, okay? Because this isn't just about you. I'm trying to figure something out.

Pam: Proceed with caution.

Jill: I want to tell you something and when I'm done I want you to tell me if there is any accuracy to it. I want you to promise in advance that you will answer me, one; and two, you'll answer me honestly.

Pam: Are you coming out or something?

Jill: Pam.

Pam: Sorry. Anything's possible.

Jill: Will you answer me honestly?

Pam: Yes, honey, of course I will.

Jill: When I look at this bowl, I get an immediate feeling in my gut and an impression in my mind. I feel like you were thinking of your mother while you were making it. I feel like you had a strong impulse to make a whole series of bowls, as a visual memoir of your mother, but you were afraid that people would start to dissect you and your mother. And you decided not to, rather than expose your memory of her to careless strangers. Art critics, agents, and the like. Am I nuts or have you had that thought?

Pam: What is this?

Jill: Please Pam, just answer the question.

Pam: Are you fucking with me?

Jill: No, honey, I promise. I wouldn't screw around with something like this…

Pam: How the fuck could you know that?

Jill: It's accurate then?

Pam: Exactly. How do you know that?

Jill: I'm not sure. Something is happening to me. I get the same feeling and impression every time I come in here and see that bowl. I also noticed you hadn't sent it over to the store to be sold.

Pam: It's a beautiful series. I've seen them all. All the bowls. What I see in my head is so beautiful, I'm afraid to even try to make them. I'm afraid I can't make them the way I see them. I feel like there is a part of Mom that I never knew, or never realized I knew, that is in the images of the bowls.

Jill: Oh my lord, even the details are the same.

Pam: You haven't answered my question.

Jill: I'm knowing things and I don't know how or why. It feels deep, and right and so incredibly beautiful, but I can't for the life of me figure out why it's happening.

Pam:	I feel like I'm absolutely supposed to do the series with the bowls. But I also feel an intense resistance to it. I mean, really intense. I know I could not do it, even though I feel that there's a really good, if unclear reason to do it.
Jill:	I know how you feel. There's a reason for this, but part of me would just as soon not know. If I were to say yes to this, whatever it is, it feels like there's no turning back.
Pam:	Exactly. And if I do this thing with the bowls, I will have said something that can't be unsaid and my life will change forever.
Jill:	I think it already has.
Pam:	Cut it out.
Jill:	I'm not trying to be weird. I don't think either one of us can stop what's happening. Even though we don't know exactly where it is leading.
Pam:	What the hell made you decide to bring this up now?
Jill:	I had to. I've almost brought it up a couple of times, but I chickened out.
Pam:	I feel a little naked. What else do you think you know about me?
Jill:	It's not like that. It's the damn bowl. It's like it's talking to me. I can't explain it.
Pam:	What the hell are we supposed to do now?
Jill:	Beats me. I think I just did what I'm supposed to do. Like I was supposed to hit you on the head and say "pay attention".
Pam:	I don't know if I have the guts to do it.
Jill:	Hey, if I found the guts to bring it up, you can find the guts to do the bowls.
Pam:	No turning back, huh?
Jill:	No turning back.

Walking In Footsteps

Premise: **Meredith** I am a woman, she is a woman; we have a relationship, she is my sister. We are in a restaurant.

                Linda I am a woman, she is a woman; we have a relationship, she is my sister. We are in a restaurant.

Meredith:	Sorry I'm late. God, what a day.
Linda:	How's it going?
Meredith:	Slow. Getting a lot of resistance. Male dominated house and senate. They just don't have clear priorities. Education is still at the bottom of the list.
Linda:	Maybe you're barking up the wrong tree.
Meredith:	Meaning?
Linda:	Perhaps there are other aspects of education, which would get the attention of the men on the Hill. Fighting for one language in the schools strikes me as too controversial for most legislators. And besides, there are other aspects of education, which are really more important.
Meredith:	Oh, please, Linda. You sound like every man I speak to on the Hill. It has to happen, you know that. There's no way to develop a strong educational system and satisfy every different ethnic group. It's like rebuilding the tower of Babel. The U.S. can never compete in the world market if we weaken our educational system even more than it is. It isn't fair to our children to leave them unprepared for the world they're going to inherit.
Linda:	Meredith, get off your soapbox. I want to have lunch; I don't want to be lobbied.
Meredith:	Then why'd you bring it up?
Linda:	I didn't, you did. You sound frustrated.
Meredith:	You can't possibly imagine.

Linda:	What am I, a Martian? I have kids in school too. I care what kind of education they get.
Meredith:	I mean what it's like on the Hill. Our kids will be out of school before we get any significant changes initiated. You can't be complacent. The system won't change itself.
Linda:	Meredith, I know that. For God's sake, don't treat me like an idiot. I happen to think there are other more important things to focus on than making English the national language. It's supremist and imperialist. If you weren't so invested in your Ivy League education, you'd see what children really need.
Meredith:	For Christ's sake. You're still jealous because I got a scholarship to Harvard. You're pitiful. I earned the right to study there and I will not apologize for it.
Linda:	You are so fucking arrogant. I'm not jealous. I got the kind of education I wanted. I'm happy and I'm happy for you. But I don't want what you want and you act like I'm defective because of it. I don't care about your scholarship. Do you get it? It's the least important thing in my life.
Meredith:	Then why do you get so angry when the subject comes up?
Linda:	It's not your degree. Not directly. It's this upper middle class intellectual attitude you've taken on. We're Jews, Meredith. It's dangerous. Someone else thought pure white was best. One race, one language, what's the difference? I can't believe you could buy into such a belief. That's what upsets me.
Meredith:	What are you saying? I think like a Nazi? I have not forgotten that I'm a Jew. That's why I want our kids to have a chance.
Linda:	We're not exactly living in a shtetl. You and I have had it pretty good.
Meredith:	I don't think our public schools are preparing our kids for the real world.
Linda:	If you want your kids to have something of value, let them learn to accept people on their own terms. Let them learn to respect someone's need for their own cultural heritage. Whether it's Korean, Central American, Vietnamese, African, Irish, Muslim, or Jewish. Let them learn to live together with their differences. If you try to wipe out the differences you're one step away from being a Nazi, Jew or no Jew.
Meredith:	It's just not practical.
Linda:	No, it's not. It's human. Meredith, there is no one language that belongs on this continent. If there was, it would be a native language, but which one? Lots of nations of people were here long before us. Which language do we use? The language of the

conqueror? That's how history gets rewritten. That's how crimes of genocide are hidden.

Meredith: Shit. You're one hell of an advocate.

Linda: I'm a Jew. And a woman and a mother. I know what matters to me.

Meredith: I'm playing right into the system. Good God!

Linda: Don't worry about the system so much. Think of the people. We're all in this together.

Meredith: Collective judgment is wrong. Elie Wiesel said that. "All collective judgments are wrong. Only racists make them," is what he says. Never thought of myself as a racist. So innocent, so insulated, so righteous. So sure of myself as I fight to make the past the future. It's how we do it, isn't it? So subtle, so insidious. This has been a sobering lunch.

Linda: We haven't even ordered yet.

Meredith: Let's quit while we're ahead. I'd rather take a walk. Is that okay with you?

Linda: It's fine. Let's go.

Meredith: I'm glad you're my sister. You got a good head. You know that?

Linda: You're not patronizing me, are you?

Meredith: No way. You've been the standard by which I've judged myself my whole life.

Linda: So you have been competing with me.

Meredith: With myself really.

What A Day

Premise:　**May** I am a woman, she is a woman; we have a relationship, she is my friend. We are at her house.

Jane I am a woman, she is a woman; we have a relationship, she is my friend. We are at my house. Grandmother died this morning.

May: Jesus, what a screwed up day. I swear to whatever it's best to swear to. Christ, Mohammed, Moses, Buddha, Krishna, my Uncle Zack. Whoever will listen. This has been a day to top them all.

Jane: What happened?

May: What didn't. My alarm goes off. I jump out of bed. My cat has had diarrhea right there, where I step. Bare feet in cat diarrhea. First thing in the morning.

Jane: Bad start.

May: Gets worse. The phone immediately starts ringing. I hop over to it on one foot, but I have too much momentum going, I lose my balance and crash into the phone stand sending the goddamned phone into the corner behind the chair. I'm trying to move the chair and pick up the phone balancing on one foot and hoping I won't vomit from the stench. The phone, of course, is off the hook, so I know whoever is calling can hear everything that's going on. I want to jump out the window.

Jane: Who was it?

May: Jerry. The clients who were due in at 1:00 had to change flights and were getting in at ten and wanted to meet right away. We, of course, weren't ready. So a working breakfast turned into working coffee and danish and a Xerox marathon at Copy King.

Jane: How'd the meeting go?

May: Insane. The clients had to forego breakfast in order to get their plane. They were hungry and cranky. We ordered lox and bagels and coffee. It took forever. We were so hungry when the food came, and so pressed for time, that we decided to eat and talk at the same time. Mr. Chan was trying to ask a question while trying to swallow too big a piece of lox and bagel and choked. Got it jammed deep in his throat, he's wheezing and turning reddish blue. Jerry had to do the Heimlich on him and broke one of his ribs. The meeting was officially over when the paramedics took Chan to the hospital.

Jane: Jesus, I hope you took the rest of the day off.

May: No dice. I smoothed my hair, adjusted my jacket and turned to go back to the conference room and Mr. Falbrook, Chan's Euro-partner, says, "Do you think we could continue the meeting this afternoon?" He was so sweet and so sincere that I thought, "Did he miss what just happened?" Well, it struck me funny and I started to laugh and I couldn't stop. Every time I tried to speak I'd hiss, and when I tried to breathe I'd wheeze. He looked at me like I was something from the seventh level of hell and I ran to the bathroom. Jerry had to smooth things over. How was your day?

Jane: I'm almost afraid to tell you. Just about everyone's here for the weekend. Jack's picking up Sue and Brad right now. This is one of the biggest things I've ever planned and it's gone real well, the party tonight, the picnic and rafting tomorrow. It was the only way to get the younger ones to come to Grandmother's ninetieth.

May: Is she excited?

Jane: Well, she was.

May: What happened?

Jane: She died.

May: She what?

Jane: This morning at 7:14 she died. Said she felt a little dizzy, sat down and died. Right there on my couch. Dead.

May: Jesus, Jane, why did you let me go on like I did?

Jane: I was enjoying the recess.

May: Why didn't you say something?

Jane: How?

May: I feel like shit.

Jane: Don't. Frankly, no matter what you'd have said I was feeling very tense and awkward about having to announce it.

May: I am so sorry. What a shock!

Jane: Luckily, my aunt and uncle got here yesterday and Mom and Dad and all of them took us out to dinner last night, so Grandma had a very nice time. She was so happy to see everyone. I am so unnerved about how to tell everyone else, "Hi, thanks for coming.

	Instead of a birthday party we're gonna have a funeral." I can't believe it happened this way.
May:	Well, in a way it's very poetic. She got to be together with her kids and you and Jack. You have to look at it positively.
Jane:	I don't want to be the one to tell everyone else, my cousins, the kids. It doesn't make sense, but I feel like The Grinch Who Stole Christmas.
May:	Honey, you didn't kill her. She just died. You're not responsible. Let Jack tell the others, or your uncle. You don't have to do it.
Jane:	I suppose.
May:	Look. Take this as a sign. Your Grandmother's spirit was ready. There's something right and wonderful in this. You're just in shock. A little more than normal because you're all geared up to host a big party tonight. You were set for it. It's just not going to happen the way you expected.
Jane:	You can say that again. The mood's sure switched. Should I still have the party?
May:	Yes, of course. Make it a special wake just for the family. Celebrate her life, just the way you'd planned.
Jane:	I had all these special little surprises planned for her. I feel a little robbed. Isn't that selfish?
May:	No. It's normal. Look honey, you are going to have to back up a little. Give yourself time to switch gears. The first thing you need to do is get it, that you're not giving the party you thought you were. It just ain't happenin'.
Jane:	Seems like a dream I can't quite figure out.
May:	You have to say to yourself, "Grandma is gone now. How do I feel about that?" Just focus on that. That's what you'd be doing if it were any other day.
Jane:	She was so well yesterday. She was so cute at the hairdresser. Joking around, making fun of getting so much attention. I just can't believe she's gone.
May:	Thank providence that you were able to make her last day on earth so happy. You've been given a gift. You'll see that eventually.
Jane:	I do. I see it. Through the fog, dimly. Will you come to the party tonight? I'll feel more sane if you're there.
May:	Sure. A perfect ending to a perfectly indescribable day. A birthday party-wake oughta finish me off just fine.
Jane:	It's not what you're in the mood for, I'm sure.
May:	I don't know…life, death, eternity. They kind of put Mr. Chan into perspective. I'll be glad to be there with you.

Male/Male Scenes

Bury The Dead

Premise: **Jeff** I am a man, he is a man; we have a relationship, he is my brother. We are in his home. Dad's funeral was today.

Peter I am a man, he is a man; we have a relationship, he is my brother. We are in my home. Dad's funeral was today

Jeff: How does it feel?

Peter: It? Could you be a little more specific? Just what is the it?

Jeff: Jesus, why are you so touchy? I thought it was fairly obvious.

Peter: Well, let's see. We just buried Dad. How does it feel to put him in the ground. How does it feel with him gone? How does it feel to be in the same room with you? You see, it's not fairly obvious, there are a lot of choices.

Jeff: You left out the one I was referring to. How does it feel to be in charge now? To know you can run things the way you want to.

Peter: You are amazing. I know you think you're pretty damned smart, but you're pretty damned stupid really. It's awesome how successful stupid people can become.

Jeff: Don't start a fight, Peter. I thought you'd be relieved to finally be able to run the business the way you want. Dad was a control freak. No big secret.

Peter: I feel just peachy, Jeff. Don't you worry about me. In fact, I'm sorry you're leaving so soon, you'll miss the celebration.

Jeff: What are you talking about?

Peter: I've planned a private ceremony. I thought I'd burn Dad's desk and all his other solid oak office furniture. Out with the old, in with the new.

Jeff: Why are you so angry? Did I do something?

Peter:	No, Jeff. You did nothing. Sure you can't leave tonight? Do you have to wait till tomorrow? I mean, wouldn't it be more convenient for you to leave now?
Jeff:	I thought we'd have a chance to talk, now that the funeral is behind us. Obviously, I was wrong. What is it you blame me for?
Peter:	Nothin', we're just different, you and me. You see things the way it's easiest to see them. You don't know me. You look at me, but you don't see me. You see what you want to see.
Jeff:	I see you pretty clearly. I see a man who is angry. Angry because you gave up your life trying to prove something to a father who was never, never gonna see you for who you are.
Peter:	Thanks, I feel a lot better now.
Jeff:	Dad never did anything to anyone or for anyone unless it was to satisfy his own ego. Including jerking you around like a puppet.
Peter:	Get out of here. Get the hell out.
Jeff:	Get it straight, little brother. You are angry with Dad, not me. But you've put it on me ever since I left here. Grow up, get over it. I don't need to be blamed and hated for living my life the best I know how. We don't ever have to see each other again. Dad's dead, there's no more family. So if that's what you want, just say so.
Peter:	I've got demons, Jeff. I can't stop them. They confuse me. I know it's wrong to feel what I'm feeling. I know there's another better feeling out there. I don't know which way to reach. It all seems like blackness.
Jeff:	Let him go, Peter. Dad was a stupid mean son of a bitch. He lived life the only way he knew how. You couldn't see what I saw. I don't know why I knew it, but I knew he'd never change. You kept thinking one day he'd give you the respect you deserve. He didn't. And now he's dead. And now you've got to live.
Peter:	I don't think I know how. I lived my whole life covering up for Dad. Making excuses for him. Fearing him, wanting him to love me. Hating him for not loving me. Hating you for being free. I'm scared, Jeff.
Jeff:	Me too, every day of my life.
Peter:	You want to know how nutty I am? My biggest fear was, that one day he'd just come right out and tell me what he thought of me.
Jeff:	Which would have been what?
Peter:	That he didn't love me – that he didn't really even like me. That it didn't matter that I was his son. That I was just another person he could manipulate.
Jeff:	Peter.

Peter:	It seemed like that. The few times he ever looked right at me the look on his face said that. That he just wished I'd go away. I was convinced that he would actually say it one day.
Jeff:	He hated himself, not you.
Peter:	The result is the same.
Jeff:	Yeah. I can't argue with that.
Peter:	No you can't.
Jeff:	Okay if I stay through tomorrow?
Peter:	Yeah sure, I'll keep my demons in their cage. No actually, honestly, I'd really like it if you stayed. I hope you know I mean it.
Jeff:	I do.

Fishing in L.A.

Premise: **Lenny** I am a man, he is a man; we have a relationship, I'm his producer.

Bobby I am a man, he is a man; we have a relationship, he is my producer.

Lenny: Bobby, where are you going?

Bobby: Fishing.

Lenny: Very funny.

Bobby: Keep laughing. See you later.

Lenny: Cut it out.

Bobby: I just don't feel like singing today.

Lenny: You better start feeling like it. I've got Studio A full of musicians and we're ready to record. Take a break and get over whatever it is.

Bobby: If I don't want to sing today, I'm not singing. Plain and simple. Tell them all to go home.

Lenny: What's the matter, you need to get laid or something? Is that it?

Bobby: Are you really as simple as you appear to be?

Lenny: Watch your mouth.

Bobby: You haven't got a clue. I gotta go.

Lenny: You can't do this.

Bobby: Watch me.

Lenny: You got a contract.

Bobby: What about it?

Lenny: You're violating it.

Bobby: My contract says I gotta sing even when I got laryngitis?

Lenny: No.

Bobby: I got laryngitis. "La". See, I can't sing a note.

Lenny:	Why are you doing this to me? I've got schedules to meet. I got you the best damn studio musicians in the city.
Bobby:	I don't want studio musicians.
Lenny:	It's the union – you've got to use 'em. Don't make trouble – it'll come back on you, I swear.
Bobby:	Are you threatening me?
Lenny:	I'm telling you how it is. I don't make the rules.
Bobby:	The rules are fucking me up. I can't sit down with a bunch of guys I've never met and just put together a song. I don't work that way.
Lenny:	This isn't a barn in Tennessee. This is a multi-million dollar recording business.
Bobby:	I don't think it's for me. You take away my band – the guys who helped me make my music – and you put me in a glass booth with a studio full of strangers playing instruments I've never seen and you tell me to make my music. That's not my music. I don't know whose it is, but it's not mine and I can't do it your way.
Lenny:	It's a lot of new stuff for you. It's just nerves you've got. A little stage fright. You'll get used to it. You'll see.
Bobby:	No. I know stage fright. I feel that every night before I go on. In the studio it's…I'm dead in there.
Lenny:	Okay, okay. What do you want? Jesus! I'm probably going to lose my job. Tell me what you need.
Bobby:	My band. I need my band. I need Donnie and Dave and Pee-Wee. That's what I need.
Lenny:	That's it? That's all you need? Alright. Tell me where to reach them.
Bobby:	Can't reach 'em right now.
Lenny:	Can they fly out tonight?
Bobby:	That's awful short notice.
Lenny:	We have got to start recording.
Bobby:	Relax. You're sweatin'. What time is it?
Lenny:	10:30. Why?
Bobby:	Gosh, I'm gonna be late. Their plane's due in at eleven. I gotta go. Today they get the music. Tomorrow we rehearse. Thursday we record.
Lenny:	Alright, alright, whatever you say. Oh man, this better work.

Goodbye MacDougal

Premise: **One** I am a man, he is a man; we have a relationship, we work together. We are at work.

                 Two I am a man, he is a man; we have a relationship, we work together. We are at work. MacDougal is dead.

One:	Hey, what's up?
Two:	My dog died.
One:	Damn, sorry to hear it. What happened.
Two:	Poison.
One:	Somebody poisoned your dog?
Two:	No. He just ate something that was poison.
One:	Man, that would be awful if someone poisoned your dog.
Two:	Well nobody did, so just shut up.
One:	Sorry, it was just when you first said it, that's what I thought you were saying.
Two:	Will you shut the fuck up, please?
One:	Okay…Okay… Sorry.
Two:	And stop sayin' you're sorry. "I'm sorry, I'm sorry." Don't you know any other words?
One:	Sorry.
Two:	I'm gonna fuckin' kill you.
One:	Get a grip, will you. It's a very sad thing that your dog died. I'm just tryin' to say the right thing.
Two:	Well, the right thing is nothing. Just say nothing. You honor the dead with silence, so just shut up.
One:	Okay…For how long?
Two:	'Til I tell you.

One: Okay.

(They sit still for a moment)

Two: He was the best thing that ever happened in my life. I'm sorry I yelled at you. I just don't know how to handle this. He was the first good thing that ever happened to me. Hell, the only good thing. You know what?

One: What?

Two: I'm mad at him.

One: Who?

Two: MacDougal, my dog.

One: Why?

Two: For dying...makin' me feel this way. It hurts. Think it's okay to be mad at someone who is dead?

One: I hope so. I been mad at my Dad for ten years. That's how long he's been dead.

Two: Didn't know your Dad was dead, sorry.

One: Yeah, well. It's been ten years. I should be over it.

Two: No you shouldn't. I don't want to be over it. Right now, there's me and MacDougal. Even if it hurts, at least there's something. If I get over it, what will there be? Nothin'. There will be nothin'.

One: Yeah, I know what you mean. I can't imagine what comes after being angry. So I stay mad.

Two: He wasn't a good father?

One: He wasn't bad. He just never...I don't know what he never did, but I didn't know him really. Then he died. No answers, no conclusions...just gone.

Two: Bummer.

One: Yeah, big bummer.

Two: Sorry that happened to you.

One: Sorry your dog died.

Neuro Impudence

Premise: **Huntsworth** I am a man, he is a man; we have a relationship, he is a professor in my department at the university. We are in my office.

Jansen I am a man, he is a man; we have a relationship, he is the Dean of my department, at the university where I teach. We are in his office.

Huntsworth: Good morning, Professor Jansen.

Jansen: Dean Huntsworth.

Huntsworth: Thank you for coming in early. Our schedules seem to do nothing but get more hectic.

Jansen: Yes, it seems so.

Huntsworth: The second class hasn't been too much this semester?

Jansen: Second?

Huntsworth: Yes. We added a second. This semester.

Jansen: Oh, the honors class, yes. I mean no. It is not too much.

Huntsworth: Everything else alright?

Jansen: What's it to ya?

Huntsworth: Excuse me?

Jansen: Sure. Whatever.

Huntsworth: Steve. May I call you Steve?

Jansen: You can call me Mary, I don't give a shit. Just get to the point.

Huntsworth: What point would that be?

Jansen: Don't be coy with me, Huntsworth.

Huntsworth: Please explain yourself.

Jansen: Inte-frickin'-lectuals.

Huntsworth: Professor Jansen. I am trying very hard to not take your casualness personally. Are you having a problem? Is there something you need to get off your chest, as it were?

Jansen: Off my chest as it were. It were? You mean it as it was. Damn confusing language, wouldn't you say?

Huntsworth: It's a phrase, an idiom, that's all. Professor, should I call a doctor?

Jansen: Not a bad idea. It would take a surgeon to dissect your sentences.

Huntsworth: Are you angry with me? I can't tell if you're being hostile or incoherent. Please tell me. Is everything all right with you?

Jansen: No. I'm having a little difficulty.

Huntsworth: With what, exactly?

Jansen: Neuro impeders.

Huntsworth: Neuro impeders?

Jansen: Mine. They've abandoned me, the unthankful bastards. I don't think about what I'm about to say. I just say it. It's usually blunt and often sarcastic. It's as though I know what I've said only after I've said it. Not before. It strikes me that knowing what one is saying before one says it would be much better if one is a teacher. Professor of Neuropsychology at an instigation of higher learning, like this old dinosaur.

Huntsworth: I don't know what to make of this. I don't know how to proceed.

Jansen: 'Tis not yours to do 'tis mine me fears, 'tis mine.

Huntsworth: How's that?

Jansen: Don't be a tree stump. You're the Dean. The Dean Supreme. Use your old noggin. Put me out to pasture.

Huntsworth: I don't want to.

Jansen: How good of you. But goodness is immaterial at the moment. My brain is misfunctioning, malfunctioning, whatever the hell the correct term is. My neuro impeders aren't working. And it's causing a bit of neuro impudence, wouldn't you say? I don't mean to be mean. Same damn word, two different definitions. You need a dictionary just to get down the hall in this place. Sorry. See. Brain is gone. For all practical purposes.

Huntsworth: We'll do a medical on you. I want you back, Jansen.

Jansen: Me too.

Huntsworth: I hope you'll trust me. I'll oversee this personally.

Jansen: That's good of you, but I don't know if there's much point.

Huntsworth: Is there anyone I can call in your family to alert them to what we're facing?

Jansen: Yes, let's face it. Is that what you asked me?

Huntsworth: A family member. Someone to include in this from your end.

Jansen: My end? This is the end. My only friend, the end.

Huntsworth: Steve. Do you understand what I just asked you?

Jansen: Yes.

Huntsworth: Do you want me to call someone in your family?

Jansen: Do you think it's fair? I mean, it might upset her.

Huntsworth: Who?

Jansen: Melanie. My fiancée. This will scare her.

Huntworth: She'll be concerned, naturally. As I am. But she'll want to be informed.

Jansen: Informed. She's quite well formed. Do you mean encased? She won't like that. She's a bit of a free-spirit.

Huntsworth: Is there a number where I can reach her?

Jansen: It's why I love her, you know.

Huntsworth: How's that?

Jansen: She's free-spirited. She lifts me up.

Huntsworth: That's a good thing, isn't it? To have someone like that in your life.

Jansen: Yes.

Huntsworth: Can you give me her number?

Jansen: Here. It's her business card. I've been carrying it in case something happens. In case I get encased. I'll tell you, this is exhausting.

Huntsworth: What is?

Jansen: Having a run-away brain.

Huntsworth: I imagine it is.

Jansen: You've imagined it? No. It's real. Quite real.

Huntsworth: Steve, try to relax. This could be just a temporary chemical imbalance. I'm going to call Melanie now, and then the University Hospital. I'll go there with you.

Jansen: You da boss, Dean. You da boss.

Russia In G

Premise: **Gregor** I am a man, my name is Gregor. I am in my home.

Tchaikowski I am a man, he is a man; we are meeting for the first time. We are in his home.

Gregor: Good God.

Tchaikowski: Don't be alarmed.

Gregor: I was completely alone a moment ago. Have you come to take me?

Tchaikowski: Quite the contrary.

Gregor: Then I've lost my wits and I'm talking to my own projection.

Tchaikowski: Not exactly.

Gregor: Don't toy with me.

Tchaikowski: Do I look like a specter of death?

Gregor: No. No you don't.

Tchaikowski: Then you don't mind if I stay?

Gregor: Ach. No, stay if you must. Clearly I haven't much say in it.

Tchaikowski: It's up to you.

Gregor: Up to me. It is odd to hear you say that. Here, where all is decided for us. Even for poets. What we can express, whom we may speak to, whom we must address and how.

Tchaikowski: I too am a Russian.

Gregor: You're not a communist.

Tchaikowski: No, I'm not.

Gregor: You travel alone and you come and go as you please.

Tchaikowski: The laws of man cannot stop God's will. When I walked this earth, men were governed by a different set of rules. Some accepted it, some didn't. You are a poet and a Russian.

Gregor: Who are you?

Tchaikowski: My name is Peter.

Gregor: Peter the Great?

Tchaikowski: No.

Gregor: Are you a Romanoff?

Tchaikowski: No.

Gregor: There are many Peters in Russian history. I could be guessing forever.

Tchaikowski: Peter Illiaich Tchaikowski.

Gregor: Peter Illiaich. Tchaikowski... Ahhh, you speak of a much different Russia. That Russia is long gone. You would not recognize the Russia of today.

Tchaikowski: Gregor, Gregor. Your blood and my blood, it's the same. Your spirit and my spirit are stirred by the same issues.

Gregor: What possible similarities can there be? Your life was golden. Life in Russia today is gray. Why are you here? Surely you have given mankind the best a man could give.

Tchaikowski: There is more to the universe than mankind and always more to learn. As a man, I took my own life.

Gregor: You died of the plague.

Tchaikowski: I exposed myself to it. I wished to die.

Gregor: Any great artist is burdened. Burdened by his mortal limitations. Ten times more vulnerable to his own defects than the average man.

Tchaikowski: I'm here to disabuse you of that idea. You have no real burden in your human life. There is unlimited potential.

Gregor: Please go away. You depress me.

Tchaikowski: I am sorry.

Gregor: Perhaps in your magical state that is true.

Tchaikowski: What I am saying is that it is true at all times at nearly every level of creation.

Gregor: You've never experienced a bureaucracy, have you?

Tchaikowski: Dear poet, it is only a matter of perception.

Gregor: I know that I shall not see my dreams fulfilled in this life. This is not a misconception.

Tchaikowski: To perceive life as finite is.

Gregor: Don't tell me this.

Tchaikowski: I thought I could leave this world before my life had run its course. I saw only pain and suffering in my future. The mortal experience is but a part of a wonderful, endless journey.

Gregor: The deprivation of this existence starves me. I feel the life drain from me a little each day.

Tchaikowski: And yet you live. You are a poet. A great poet. You have a voice, which Russians hear. If your present governors take away the light, you must celebrate the dark.

Gregor: You come from a different time. You do not know.

Tchaikowski: During my life there were Russians who lived in darkness. That was their experience. At times I was among them. If your governors take away the music, if they take away all that is sweet and all that remains is a bitter wind then, poet, you must celebrate the trembling of a leaf, the bending of a blade of grass.

Gregor: A leaf, a blade of grass. These are insignificant when whole nations of people are denied life.

Tchaikowski: People lose their way when the leaf and the bloom are no longer important to them. There is life and energy all around you. What is more powerful than a Russian blizzard or the silence which surrounds you when the storm is over and all is absorbed in frozen drifts.

Gregor: You, Peter Illiaich. You are the poet. Why have you come to me?

Tchaikowski: You have a voice, which Russians listen for.

Gregor: I am one voice crying out amidst the droning of millions. I think I would rather be with you in the realms of light.

Tchaikowski: You cannot do what you have to do from where I am. You have the means to transform your world. There is power, which comes from the land. You must open yourself to it; don't weep it away. You can create a world of light right where you are. A world of such light that no government could rule it away. This is the world that lives now in your heart.

Gregor: I feel my heart shall break for all that I want for Russia and for myself.

Tchaikowski: Your heart will break a thousand times if you are brave enough to let it. Each time it shatters, its pieces tell a story.

Gregor: All that Russia ever was or is, is in me. She is mine and I am hers. Her people are here, here in my heart. The golden Russia I see is not just a fantasy.

Tchaikowski: That is the Russia that pure love sees. The rest is an illusion.

Summer Void

Premise: **Steve**   am a man, he is a man; we have a relationship, he is my younger brother. We are at home.

                Robbie I am a man, he is a man; we have a relationship, he is my older brother. We are at home.

Steve:	Robbie, do you have the car keys?
Robbie:	Yeah, I'm using the car tonight. I told Mom that.
Steve:	Can't you get one of your friends to drive?
Robbie:	No.
Steve:	I need the car tonight.
Robbie:	Where are ya goin'?
Steve:	Tori Amos. You goin' out with Skip?
Robbie:	No. He's got band practice.
Steve:	Oh, you have a date?
Robbie:	Never mind. It isn't important. Here are the damn keys.
Steve:	What's with you?
Robbie:	Nothin'. What's with you? I gave you the keys.
Steve:	I thought you said you had plans.
Robbie:	I didn't say I had plans.
Steve:	Well, why do you need the car?
Robbie:	So I can get out of here.
Steve:	Where to?
Robbie:	Cruise around. Nothin' special.
Steve:	Is that what you've been doing every night? Does Skip go with you?
Robbie:	No.

Steve: Buzzy and Brad?

Robbie: I don't hang out with them anymore.

Steve: Dan?

(Robbie says nothing.)

Steve: What happened Robbie? Where are all your friends?

Robbie: Beats me.

Steve: Did something happen?

Robbie: No.

Steve: Fight? Girlfriend thing?

Robbie: No.

Steve: Well, what?

Robbie: Well, what what?

Steve: You don't just stop being friends one day.

Robbie: How do you know? It happens.

Steve: Maybe with one friend, sometimes, but not all your buds at once.

Robbie: Shows what you know.

Steve: Are you tellin' me you all decided one day to not be friends anymore?

Robbie: Butt out, Dr. Phil.

Steve: I don't believe this. I'm callin' Skip.

Robbie: Do not call Skip.

Steve: There's got to be a reason for this.

Robbie: Oh, big college man – gonna figure it out? Gonna fix it? You're not Dad. You can't fix everything.

Steve: What is the matter with you?

Robbie: You're the matter with me.

Steve: What'd I do?

Robbie: I gave you the keys, will you get outta here!

Steve: I just don't get it that's all. This should be a great summer for you. You're outta high school. Soon you'll be at college.

Robbie: Or not.

Steve: What?

Robbie: There's no reason for me to go.

Steve: Since when?

Robbie: I'm not like you and Ray.

Steve: Ray and me are not that alike.

Robbie: You know what you want to be. What you want to do.

Steve:	Oh. What's this got to do with you and your friends?
Robbie:	They do too. It's all they talk about. Everyone's so ready to just forget everything and move on.
Steve:	Too fast for you?
Robbie:	I'm not in a hurry to leave everything behind.
Steve:	Well, you don't really leave it behind-behind. I'm back, aren't I?
Robbie:	For six or eight weeks. But where do you really live?
Steve:	This is still home.
Robbie:	It is?
Steve:	Look, you're gonna be all into your architecture. You won't have time to look back.
Robbie:	Yay.
Steve:	You're gonna be an architect man. How cool is that?
Robbie:	I don't know. Maybe it's not a good idea.
Steve:	Not a good idea? Mr. Robbie Lloyd Wright. Ming Cho Robbie. C'mon man, it's your thing.
Robbie:	I don't want to go.
Steve:	Oh, well then… Can I ask you something?
Robbie:	Could I stop you?
Steve:	I just want you to know, if you're scared, I understand.
Robbie:	Asshole.
Steve:	I was scared before I went.
Robbie:	Oh please, you were not. You couldn't wait to go.
Steve:	Yes and no. I was scared, but you know what?
Robbie:	Please tell me, oh great wise one.
Steve:	It's just a bunch of kids – just like you and me and Skip. Tryin' to figure out how to organize themselves. Everybody's lost at sea at first.
Robbie:	Really.
Steve:	Really.
Robbie:	You're livin' with a bunch of people you don't know. That's bogus.
Steve:	Yeah, it's a little weird at first. But you get to know them.
Robbie:	What if I get a jerk roommate.
Steve:	It happens.
Robbie:	Great.
Steve:	You can request a change. The school is set up for most situations. It's not as bad as you think.

Robbie:	I could get a job.
Steve:	At the Gas n' Go. Now there's a future.
Robbie:	Shut up.
Steve:	You can't design cool buildings with a gas pump in your hand. Come on Robbie – you've just got the willies. It's normal.
Robbie:	Why do you have to be right all the time?
Steve:	I don't have to be. I just am. This time. Tell me you have not acted this way with all your friends.
Robbie:	No. I'm just avoiding them.
Steve:	Well get on the horn and hook up with 'em. Do somethin' – do nothin', it doesn't matter, just do it with someone. Don't be alone.
Robbie:	Yeah, yeah, yeah. Okay.
	(Steve looks at him.)
Robbie:	No really. Okay. I get it.
Steve:	Okay. Good. See ya later.
Robbie:	Later.

This Life

Premise: **Mike** I am a man, he is a man; we are meeting for the first time. We are on the sidewalk in Santa Monica.

                Stu I am a man, he is a man; we are meeting for the first time. We are on the sidewalk in Santa Monica. I have been drinking.

Mike:	You look like you could use a meal.
Stu:	I haven't slept. That's my problem. Can't sleep. I don't really need any food. What I need is sleep.
Mike:	How'd you get off the track.
Stu:	No one wants…well…I'm alone a lot. That gets on your nerves.
Mike:	When did you work last?
Stu:	Three days ago. I should have kept going to work.
Mike:	Why did you stop?
Stu:	I felt like it was over so I stopped going. My real problem is that I drink. Where are you going?
Mike:	To Hollywood.
Stu:	Oh, near Ventura?
Mike:	No, Hollywood above Sunset.
Stu:	Oh. Well can you give me a lift?
Mike:	Is that where you want to go?
Stu:	Yeah sure.
Mike:	Really.
Stu:	Where are you going?
Mike:	To acting class.
Stu:	Is it open to the public?
Mike:	No. It's private.

Stu:	I guess it would have been a good idea to eat something, I haven't eaten.
Mike:	Have you been to AA?
Stu:	Oh yeah. I been there a lot. I'm so tired of the valley. All the bullshit people are so full of shit you know. I just would like to go to the beach with a bottle of wine and a baloney sandwich. Salami, salami…baloney. Remember that?
Mike:	Yeah.
Stu:	People give me so much attitude.
Mike:	People are afraid of guys like you.
Stu:	Why?
Mike:	Because you don't seem to come from anywhere and you aren't going anywhere.
Stu:	It's 'cause I smell and I'm ugly.
Mike:	You do smell and you are dirty. But you're not ugly. It's not about good or bad. It's just that most people…most people know how close they are to the edge. Crossing over the line. Like me. I work everyday so that I can take care of my car and put gas in it so I can get to work everyday, so I can take care of my car and my house. It's nutty but that's my choice. You chose something else.
Stu:	I didn't exactly choose this.
Mike:	Actually, you probably did.
Stu:	No way man, it just happened.
Mike:	Not every choice we make is a conscious one.
Stu:	Can I come to your studio?
Mike:	No.
Stu:	This is a nice car. Is it new?
Mike:	No. Go in there and get something to eat. Use this money to eat.
Stu:	Yeah, yeah.
Mike:	Look at me. What's your name?
Stu:	Stu, what's yours?
Mike:	Mike. Look at me, Stu. You promise me you'll go in there and buy something to eat. You don't eat, you die.
Stu:	Naw, I won't die.
Mike:	Yes you will. Your body can't go on nothing forever. You drink, you die.
Stu:	Okay, I'll get some ice cream. Thanks. Bye.
Mike:	Bye Stu. (*Stu leaves*). Who am I kidding? He's gonna drink. Give him a speech, Mike. That really did him a lot of good. "Wah-wah, wah-wah-wah-wah."

Non-Gender
Specific Scenes

it is my responsibility

what I do with these

amy
roemer
2011

The Bear and the Porcupine

Premise: **One**   We have a relationship, he/she is my friend.
We are lawyers on opposite sides of the same case.
We are in his/her office.

Two   We have a relationship, he/she is my friend.
We are lawyers on opposite sides of the same case.
We are in my office.

One: Can I speak with you a moment?

Two: Anything you have to say, you say in court in front of the judge.

One: Look, I don't want to be hard nosed about this, but you're making it difficult to do it any other way.

Two: Whatever way it is, is your doing. If you want it to be otherwise, then make it otherwise.

One: I am not the one charged with obstructing justice, so don't blame me for the circumstance.

Two: Why are you doing this? What's in it for you?

One: It's my job.

Two: That's simplistic.

One: Why are you being this way? You're a damn good attorney. You know what's at stake.

Two: Yeah, I know.

One: Why is this man worth wrecking your career for?

Two: Save it.

One: For Christ's sake, I'm your friend.

Two: I can't talk to you. We're on opposite sides.

One: Right now I'm on your side. I want to understand. Why are you protecting this man?

Two: Your client is the AMA. They've hired you to destroy him.

One: I don't want to destroy him.

Two:	Anything I tell you, you'll use on behalf of your client. They want him gone. I won't risk that.
One:	I'm trying to understand you. Not him. I want to know why you're doing this. I need to understand. If you don't give me something to go on, I'll go with the law and I'll bury you. I don't want that.
Two:	If you truly don't want it, don't do it.
One:	I don't have any choice.
Two:	Of course you have a choice.
One:	What choice? What choice do I have?
Two:	Recuse yourself.
One:	I can't.
Two:	You can. It's well within your ability. You won't.
One:	Why should I?
Two:	Recuse yourself because we're friends. The case right now is against me.
One:	I tell the American Medical Association I can't handle their suit because you are my friend?
Two:	This is bigger than you or me.
One:	How?
Two:	On Capital Hill the A.M is the same as the oil lobbies. It's big business. They've gotten the FDA to work as their bone crusher. Someone comes along with a cure that's accessible to everyone and the doctors and the pharmaceutical companies get the FDA to go in and shut them down. It's bad for business.
One:	You believe this guy can cure people?
Two:	Is this off the record?
One:	Yes.
Two:	Swear to me.
One:	I swear to you. Off the record.
Two:	It's not just him. It's the people who come to him. They have this trust, a mutual respect. Half of them don't even know the old ways. Most of them aren't full blooded anymore. But his presence, his way of being. They trust him. He cures them. He takes what they can give in payment.
One:	If he's curing people, they can testify. If it can be proven, then there's no case.
Two:	How can it be proven? These people have no medical records, they're poor. There's no second opinion. It's their word against the AMA. Who's going to put their professional credibility on the line when it's illiterate farm workers versus the AMA?

One: How come you care so much? How'd you get involved?

Two: You wouldn't believe me if I told you.

One: Try me.

Two: He saw me in a vision. He sent a friend to find me. I was in El Paso working a case. The guy knew everything about me, I mean little things. Personal things, things no one else could know. He said he had a friend in trouble, that he needed me. He took me to meet Don Eduardo. That's what they call him. When I arrived at his house, he was on his patio feeding a porcupine bits of cornbread.

One: A live porcupine?

Two: Not much point in feeding a dead porcupine.

One: I thought they won't let humans get near them.

Two: That's what I thought. Don Eduardo explained that when there is trust, the porcupine is a very friendly and playful animal. He looked at me and said, "I need your help. I know that I can trust you." I stayed at his house for the next two days. I watched as the people came. Like children, with complete trust and faith. He said one day, "The bear is big and gruff, it believes too much in its own cleverness. It makes the people afraid. They get sick because they believe they have no power."

One: What did he mean, "the bear"?

Two: It's a metaphor. Like the bear in a forest, the white man's government dominates with the illusion of fear. There's something blessed, sacred and wise going on in that little place, something that has to be protected at all costs. I can't explain it better than that.

One: What do you want me to do?

Two: Believe me when I tell you I'm protecting the confidentiality of my client. Don't let this case rest on a technicality. Let them lose this stage, then Don Eduardo will be safe. There's no real case against him. The case is against me, they think I'm hiding something. I'm hiding nothing. What Don Eduardo sees and does he says we all could see and do. He says it's all here for each of us, God sees no lines upon the earth. No limits upon men. Men create this illusion.

One: Alright, tomorrow I let your motion stand, I won't challenge it. If I need a job afterward, will you hire me?

Two: You want to live in west Texas?

One: Not particularly. Tell me, which animal are you? Metaphorically speaking?

Two: The porcupine.

Good News

Premise: **One** We have a relationship, he/she is my best reporter. We are in my office.

Two We have a relationship, he/she is my editor. We are in his/her office.

One: Smith? What is this?

Two: That's my article.

One: You call this reporting?

Two: Yes I do.

One: Oh you do, do you? Well I call it shit.

Two: It's what you wanted. You said you wanted something new. So that's new.

One: You have got to be joking. We're twenty minutes from deadline and you give me this for the front page. I wouldn't even print it in the weekender.

Two: Why not?

One: Why not? I'll tell you why not.

Two: No wait, let me say it, "Bad news sells newspapers".

One: That's right Smith. Now what am I going to do?

Two: The only thing you can do. Print it. I haven't got another quarter page story for the front page and there's no time to find one. Deadline, Jones. Deadline, you know. It's what makes this business so much fun.

One: Get out of here, I've got seventeen minutes left. At least I can edit it and try to make it somewhat newsworthy.

Two: What are you going to do? Change the facts? The fact is it's a nice story…It's good news. I think our readers deserve to get some good news once in a while.

One: They don't want good news. They can go to church for good news. This is a newspaper. We have to keep our ratings up. We have to print the kind of stories people want to read. Murder, rape, injustice…The end of the world. That kind of thing. A blind woman getting famous for making quilts is not front-page news.

Two: Yes it is. It shows people that there is something to be hopeful about. It shows other disabled people that they can make it in this world.

One: Oh really, Smith. What has gotten into you? You're my best reporter. What happened to that lead you had on the MIAs?

Two: We are giving the world a one-sided view. There's more to life than bad news. I don't feel like a reporter anymore. I feel like a propagandist. Keeping people in a constant state of anxiety. Jones, we could have the scoop of the century by starting to print good news on the front page.

One: I can see the headlines of our own paper: "City Gazette Fails Despite Efforts of Florence Nightingale". We'd have a good rally on the last issue.

Two: You see. It's gotten to you. You can only think negatively. Because in this business negative is positive and good is bad. It's making you crazy, Jones, and it's definitely making me crazy. I've been feeling much better for the last two weeks and you want to know why? I stopped reading our paper. Now at least I don't feel like crying until I get to the office.

One: I'm giving you a sabbatical, Smith. You've been working too hard. It's making you weird.

Two: Wrong. I've never felt better in my life. I'm just beginning to see clearly for the first time in my professional life. I like to laugh, Jones…I like to smile. I like to feel good about my fellow men and women.

One: You're sick.

Two: We can do it, Jones.

One: Why, God? Why me?

Two: I'm tellin' you, we can change the tide of modern journalism.

One: I've worked hard all my life, God.

Two: Don't be a follower.

One: Why, God?

Two: Be a leader.

One: I need this in my life?

Two: Look at this. It's tomorrow's story.

One: "Ice Cream Statues Key to Veteran's New Life".

Two: Isn't that great? Wait 'til you read it.

One:	Did somebody get to you?
Two:	It's a wonderful story. This guy had nothing to live for…
One:	Has Murdock made a deal with you? To put me out of business?
Two:	He was totally anti-social 'til he got this job at the ice cream plant.
One:	I'll be the laughing stock of editors.
Two:	I feel the tide turning, Jones – I feel it.
One:	Get out of here. I've got work to do. If I'm lucky we'll have an earthquake before press time. Nothing major, just about an eight point eight.

Showcase

Premise: **One** We have a relationship, he/she is my acting coach. We are in an empty theater.

             Two We have a relationship, he/she is my acting student. We are in an empty theater.

One: There is tyranny in my house. You can sense it if you're alert. Hanging like a pall high up in the corners of each room near the ceiling. There is treachery too. You can see it in the shadows that play tricks on you. "What?", I say. "Who is there?", but there is none. You may think me a fool to say this out loud. The others do. But they have been tyrannized and it has made them treacherous. Not to be trusted.

Two: Who are you talking to?

One: Huh?

Two: In the scene.

One: Them? Out there?

Two: Yes. Remember who they are…

One: My alter ego?

Two: Try again.

One: My conscience.

Two: Think!

One: God. It's God I'm talking to.

Two: It's not God! It's not your conscience. It's agents and casting directors. Remember that. Agents and casting directors. Don't make them guess about how you're feeling. Hit 'em right between the eyes. Understand? Now look out there. Go on, look. What do you see?

One: Chairs. Seat, lots of seats.

Two: Who is in those seats?

One:	People.
Two:	What kind of people?
One:	Nice people.
Two:	Not nice people, agents! Agents and casting directors. Don't look at me, look out there, what do you see?
One:	Agents.
Two:	And how do you feel when you see them?
One:	I don't know, I've never met one.
Two:	You love them. They get you jobs. They are your lifeline in this business. Without an agent you don't exist. What do you see?
One:	Agents.
Two:	What do you feel?
One:	Love. I love you agents. Hi! Got the big love goin' for ya.
Two:	Pick it up from where you left off.
One:	Okay… "But they have been tyrannized and it has made them treacherous. Not to be trusted." I don't understand. How am I supposed to be saying this and loving them and getting it across to them how I feel within the scene?
Two:	Just keep going.
One:	Okay. Here we go. "Once there was love here and mutual respect. Now just trickery and deceit. Ambition has poisoned the well from which we drink our life and now Mother would sooner sell son as suckle him. Brothers sleep with drawn daggers as pillows."
Two:	Alright. One of them is your brother. Find him as you speak. Let him know you love him in spite of what he's done.
One:	What did he do?
Two:	What does it say in the script?
One:	He's not in the script, he's an agent. There are no agents in the play…
Two:	You pretend that treachery and deceit is what he's guilty of, but you let him know that you can forgive him.
One:	Why can I forgive him?
Two:	Because I told you to.
One:	But I don't even know what he has done.
Two:	He's an agent. That's all you need to know. And you're willing to forgive him. Now show me everything you've got. Really put your energy out there. Remember, without an agent, you're like the proverbial tree falling in an empty forest. Okay, pick it up from where you left off and move me.

One: "My wakeful eyes trace the time-darkened ripples in plaster walls
            and memory plays itself out in steely echoes like a song learned
            but never sung. I anticipate your touch and yet it never comes.
            And here I stay prisoner in a house of fools. Taunted and teased
            and never satisfied. Reality becomes a mirage of all that could, but
            never will be. Your promises are lies and your favors are traps.
            But all this I could forgive if just once you would come out of the
            shadows and state clearly your intentions, whatever they be, so that
            I may not live my entire mortal life unknowing of your purpose."

Two: I think you're beginning to understand.

One: Yeah, I felt it. It was like the brother and the agent are all one –
            I mean subjectively, so it doesn't matter if I actually know him –
            'cause, of course I don't – or even care about him, but I felt it – it
            was real – I was really wanting to know – you know? What the
            point is. Is what I mean.

Where's the Magic?

Premise: **One** We have a relationship, we work together. He/she is a teacher. I am the principal.

Two We have a relationship, we work together; I am a teacher, he/she is my principal. We are in his/her office.

One: Your friend, the magician, has caused quite a stir.

Two: He's not really a magician.

One: It doesn't matter.

Two: Pardon?

One: I said it doesn't matter what he is.

Two: It does. Matter.

One: Not to me and not to this school. No more magic shows. Save the magic for your novels.

Two: Anything else I should save for my novels?

One: Yes.

Two: Yes?

One: Your class is Introductory Science. It's designed to give the students a general foundation in the sciences. Basic elements, action-reaction, gravity.

Two: Get to the point.

One: Some of the children have been upset about the issues you've been preaching about in your class.

Two: I don't preach.

One: Well, you've gotten pretty far off your syllabus. Look, everyone's concerned about the world becoming less safe, but this isn't the place to deal with it. You put your fantastic notions into these kids' heads and it screws them up. They're too young.

Two:	They're not too young.
One:	They're too young and their parents are calling me. They are going home and discussing these things with their parents.
Two:	I know. I told them to.
One:	You're sending them home with your opinions. That's not what we're paying you for.
Two:	Not my opinions. I teach science. Science is based on the testing of hypotheses. Nothing, not one god damned little thing has ever been discovered by accepting that what we know is all there is to know. That's science and that's what I teach.
One:	Your ideas are politically charged.
Two:	They're questions. I send them home with questions to discuss. They're not my ideas. If you don't think the hypotheses I present are possible, then tell me what is. After nuclear war, what will happen to the world, to life as we know it? What's the half-life of all the chemical weapons? How do they react to chemicals already in our urban environments? How long do they stay in the ground water? What will they do to sea life as we know it? Can you tell me? Do you know anyone, any-god-damned-one who can tell me so I don't have to worry? Who's going to figure it out?
One:	To put these questions to young people is irresponsible. You are preaching Armageddon.
Two:	They saw the towers go down. They've seen Armageddon
One:	Who consecrated you our moral arbiter?
Two:	After nuclear winter, do the trees grow back? Do birds ever fly again? Are there birds? If I'm wrong, you must know what's right? Huh? Fill me in. I'm waiting. After biological warfare, what will future homosapiens look like? I want an answer. Why so quiet? Anthrax got your tongue?
One:	Nobody can answer these questions, you know that.
Two:	Maybe I do, maybe I don't.
One:	Certainly kids can't answer them.
Two:	They won't be kids forever. What happens to your soul in a holocaust? Just tell me that?
One:	That's between me and God.
Two:	No…It's between you and me. We've got a responsibility here, you and me. Right now. I don't have the answers and I'm sure as hell not going to pretend to these kids that I do. If they don't begin to believe that they have the power to change things, then we might as well just put a gun in our mouths and pull the trigger now.

Who Cares?

Premise: **One** We have a relationship, he/she is my teacher. We are at his/her place.

Two We have a relationship, he/she is my apprentice. We are at my place.

One: You know what's interesting about cellophane? It's transparent but impermeable.

Two: Who cares?

One: I mean you can see through it but nothing can pass through it.

Two: Almost as amazing as glass.

One: No. It's different from glass because it's flexible like skin, but no moisture can pass through it.

Two: Who cares?

One: You just say "who cares" when you don't know what else to say.

Two: Who cares?

One: Will you stop it please. You're driving me crazy.

Two: Maybe you're driving yourself crazy with all your inane thoughts.

One: So what am I supposed to do? Stop thinking?

Two: It might help.

One: It might also be impossible. You're impossible. I don't know why I put up with you.

Two: Who cares?

One: That does it. I've had it. I'm leaving. You and all your damned wisdom can go rot for all I care.

Two: Are you really ready to leave? Have you attained what it was you wanted?

One: How the Hell would I know? No. I haven't. But it's not to be found here.

Two:	Oh? You know where it is then?
One:	No. I don't know where it is.
Two:	Then how do you know it's not here?
One:	Now I know why you live by yourself. No one in their right mind could endure this kind of torture.
Two:	Torture. Yes, I suppose it is something akin to torture.
One:	You suppose? You arrogant misanthrope. A true master keeps the ego out of it. You're the worst teacher I've ever had, that's what I think. So what do you think about that, huh?
Two:	Who cares?
One:	I care. I came here to learn from you and all you do is tease me and take advantage of your position.
Two:	But you do not wish to learn. I am teaching you and you have shut your ears and eyes.
One:	Oh give me a break. Do you think I traveled all this way and gave up my former life to come here and not learn?
Two:	I think you came here with a well-drawn picture of what you would find and hence you cannot see what is here. But who cares?
One:	Why did you agree to teach me, if nothing really matters to you?
Two:	I have never said that nothing matters to me. You think that your coming here was your creative act. That in just doing so the knowledge you sought would be given to you. Handed to you. You can not gain insight without illumination and there can be no illumination without an emotional charge.
	You can't sit like a lump and absorb this kind of thing. You must summon forth other levels of consciousness and this is not a passive thing. As long as you care what I think and seek my approval you will not reach those unexplored levels within yourself. To thoughts which are not part of your journey, you must say, as I say, "who cares".
One:	But how can you be part of the universe and be so isolated?
Two:	You are misinterpreting my disinterest in your mental distractions as a lack of caring. Now, you tell me, whose ego is getting in the way here?
One:	I'm sorry. This is my life we're talking about. This is my big journey, my major quest. Nothing is more important to me. I can't fail.
Two:	You are afraid of losing something that you do not yet hold in trust.
One:	I'm afraid of losing my mind.
Two:	Precisely.

One:	Precisely what?

One: Precisely what?

Two: Your mind is what you must lose.

One: Don't fuck with me.

Two: Your mind is full of a lot of misinformation. You must let that mind fall apart and form new beliefs in a clear vessel.

One: Yes. I want that.

Two: Without the new foundation present in a recognizable form, the old mind is reluctant to let die all the previous conclusions you have drawn about your life, God, the universe. So you sit in a void, not wanting to go back – not knowing how to go forward.

One: It's terrifying.

Two: That fear is blocking the pathways to deeper consciousness and heightened vision.

One: How do I know what is and isn't part of my journey.

Two: If the thoughts and perceptions you have do not excite you and make the colors around you more vivid, then those thoughts are blocking you path. You must be willing to let that part of you die. You must know the difference between preservation and creation. I think that cellophane was designed to preserve. What do you think?

One: I think you are absolutely r...—who cares?

Three Person Scenes

On My Own

Premise: **He** I am a man, she is a woman; we have a relationship, we work together. We are on our first date.

She I am a woman, he is a man; we have a relationship, we work together. We are on our first date.

Kim: Man, what a day. I don't know if I'm more hungry or more exhausted.

Mike: Would you rather go home and order out?

Kim: No, I didn't mean…no, this is nice. I want to eat here, really, I'm…just blathering. I think I'm hungry. I'll feel fine once I get something to eat. Really.

Mike: I should have thought to ask you if you were up for this.

Kim: You did.

Mike: I did?

Kim: Yeah, you said, "Wanna go out?" I said. "yes".

Mike: So you did.

Kim: This is awkward. Why do people go through this? Just because we don't know each other too well. I hate this feeling.

Mike: It's okay.

Kim: I was about to give you my three-minute social-psych analysis of our situation.

Mike: Didn't mean to cut you off.

Kim: A lucky accident then.

Mike: We can't be anywhere but where we are.

Kim: Is that your philosophy of life?

Mike: I suppose. I don't think of it as a philosophy, just reality.

Kim: Where do we get our definition of reality?

Mike: That's an awesome question.

Kim: I wish it had an awesome answer.

Mike: Life itself is the answer, don't you think?

Kim: How come everything's so okay with you? I mean is everything always so existentially okay with you?

Mike: I try not to sweat the small stuff.

Kim: Good for you. I sweat every detail. It's who I am.

Mike: Perhaps it's not.

Kim: What?

Mike: Perhaps sweating every detail isn't who you are.

Kim: Sure it is. Everybody knows that about me. It's why I keep getting promoted at work. I'm the detail person.

Mike: It might just be a choice you've made, or conditioning.

Kim: Of course. It's both. I've chosen to hone my skills.

Mike: For work?

Kim: Yes.

Mike: How about in your private life?

Kim: It's the same, if I don't deal with the details in my private life I can't deal with the shit at work.

Mike: How about me? All the details in place?

Kim: Jeez, you don't beat around the bush do you?

Mike: You think that was forward?

Kim: Forward? No. Just blunt. But I like that about you. You're so present. In the moment. Most men aren't.

Mike: That's quite a generalization.

Kim: Sorry. You know what I mean.

Mike: I didn't mean to sound critical. Sorry. I'm just trying to get to know you.

Kim: Copacetic. Refreshing actually. That's what I mean about you. You're so open and unconditional.

Mike: I have my moments, believe me.

Kim: I find that hard to imagine.

Waiter: Hi, would you like a drink?

Both: Yes.

Waiter: Okay, shoot.

Kim: Red wine, Merlot?

Waiter: Yep.

Mike: Club soda.

Waiter:	Okay.
Mike:	And an appetizer. My friend is starving. Chicken quesadilla?
Waiter:	Consider it done.
Both:	Thanks.
Kim:	What do you mean about choice or conditioning, why do you think that's different from just being yourself?
Mike:	Maybe we should change the subject. This is more middle of the night conversation.
Kim:	Come on, I'm intrigued.
Mike:	I think we often live out a condition thinking it's an unchangeable part of our nature. Or we choose to behave a certain way because we think it has a positive quality to it. Either to be sure of being accepted or to not rock the boat. If we do that we have a hard time relaxing and being real.
Kim:	I think different parts of our personalities come out in different settings.
Mike:	I think you're right about that.
Kim:	So what do you think about me?
Mike:	I'm just getting to know you.
Kim:	You must have an impression.
Mike:	I think you're very good at being a good sport. You put the group needs ahead of your own, you make....couldn't we discuss our favorite movies?
Kim:	Later. I make what?
Mike:	I don't know.
Kim:	Politely, she says, "Bullshit".
Mike:	What do I know? I don't know anything.
Kim:	Don't hedge, I'm a big girl.
Mike:	Well, at work, because that's the only place I really know you, you seem to make yourself needed by being very good at many things. And you expect to be appreciated for it.
Kim:	Zingo.
Mike:	Did you see *Shakespeare In Love*?
Kim:	And that relates to...?
Mike:	Changing the subject.
Kim:	No fair.
Mike:	Please?
Kim:	One more question. Then it's movies, I promise.
Mike:	Okay.

Kim:	What about you? What's your schtick in life?
Mike:	I'm a recovering people pleaser. I try not to buy into flattery from people or to take their bad moods personally.
Kim:	How's it going?
Mike:	Some days are better than others. But I have more serenity today than I did three years ago.
Kim:	Don't you need to be complimented, or acknowledged for what you do that's positive?
Mike:	Of course I do.
Waiter:	Sorry for the delay. Technical difficulties at the bar. Here you go. Can I get you anything else?
Mike:	We're fine for now, thanks.
Kim:	So tell me more.
Mike:	The subject is movies, you've had your one question.
Kim:	Don't be so evasive. I want to think you're different than other men.
Mike:	Generalization number two.
Kim:	Keeping score?
Mike:	I'd like not to.
Kim:	Well, certain things are true.
Mike:	And certain things are perceived or assumed, but not correctly.
Kim:	You don't date men.
Mike:	No, but I are one. Surprising that such a detail person should make such broad generalizations. You miss the uniqueness in people if you do that.
Kim:	I only meant to compliment you.
Mike:	I'm suspicious of flattery.
Kim:	Why?
Mike:	It usually has precious little to do with me.
Kim:	Sounds a little paranoid to me.
Mike:	I know. It's not really. I just know myself. I know how I used to respond to flattery and I've seen the hollowness of it, in me as well as in other people.
Kim:	What's the alternative?
Mike:	Mean what you say and say what you mean.
Kim:	Easier said than done.
Mike:	I don't live it perfectly every day.
Waiter:	Chicken quesadilla. Are you ready to order?
Mike:	No, we haven't even looked at the menu.

Waiter:	I'll give you a few more minutes. Our specials are grilled halibut with mango compote, lamb chops with mint pesto, and blackened chicken, with salsa verde.
Mike:	You want to order now?
Kim:	Sure. The halibut sounds great.
Mike:	Me too.
Waiter:	That was easy. Another round?
Both:	Sure.
Mike:	Where were we?
Kim:	One day at a time, I think. Are you an alcoholic?
Mike:	Nope. Somehow I managed not to get addicted to booze. Just work and people.
Kim:	Sounds like me.
Mike:	Sounds like ninety percent of our culture.
Kim:	Nothing special about me, huh?
Mike:	I didn't mean that.
Kim:	Of course you didn't.
Mike:	I just meant we've got company. I try to remember that other people are struggling too, so I don't judge them. So I don't resent my own problems.
Kim:	You a twelve stepper?
Mike:	Yep.
Kim:	Well, good for you.
Mike:	Is that a turn off?
Kim:	As long as you don't try to get me to a meeting.
Mike:	Wouldn't think of it.
Kim:	Do you think it's possible for two people with vastly different personalities to fall in love and have a good relationship?
Mike:	Don't know how it is with other people.
Kim:	Well, how is it with you?
Mike:	Still wondering.
Kim:	Me too.

Reunion

Premise: **Frances** I am a woman, he is a man; we are meeting for the first time. We are in my office.

Michael I am a man, she is a woman; we are meeting for the first time. We are in her office. She is a psychic medium.

Tom I am a man, he is a man; we have a relationship, he is my brother. She is a woman; we have never met. She is a psychic medium. We are in her office.

Frances:	Hello, are you Michael?
Michael:	Yes. Frances?
Frances:	Yes. We're two for two. Must be psychic.
Michael:	I thought…You knew I was coming?
Frances:	It was a joke. I saw a cartoon once. It was a picture of a waiting room. The sign on the door said, "Psychic Healing Center". On the reception desk there was another sign. It said, "Think of a number & have a seat". Relax, Michael, I'm really okay.
Michael:	I'm sorry. I'm just a little surprised. You're so normal looking.
Frances:	You expected Madame Svetlana with a gypsy skirt and wild eyes?
Michael:	No. Yes. A little. Esoteric at least, if not aboriginal. Not that I have anything against Aborigines. Oh, man.
Frances:	It's okay, really.
Michael:	I feel like I've got both feet in my mouth.
Frances:	Michael, what do you know about how I work?
Michael:	Not much. I've just heard from Jack and Sherrie that you're a psychic and you can get dead people to talk to live people, I mean dead people you love. I mean, not that you love, I mean the people who come to you. They love the dead people. Or have a connection. I mean people who are important. To each other. Shit,

why can't I talk? I'm sorry. I'm really not an idiot. I don't know what's the matter with me.

Frances: It's okay. For most people it's hard to find comfortable language to discuss these things at first. We've lost the vocabulary. Who is it you'd like to contact?

Michael: My brother Tom. Tommy. He's my younger brother.

Frances: When did he pass over?

Michael: Three years ago.

Frances: How did he die?

Michael: Motorcycle accident.

Frances: Alright. Give me a moment.

(Frances takes a few deep breaths, sits a moment. Her eyes are closed.)

Yes, I think I see him. A very handsome young man. Something was wrong when he died. It's as though he was on drugs or something. Does that seem right?

Michael: Yes.

Frances: It was a mistake, he didn't intend to die. He tried to get back in his body, but there was no way he could have been resuscitated.

Michael: Yes, his neck was broken.

Frances: He wants you to know that, although it was a tragic mistake, he is alright now.

Michael: That's what I want to know. That he's okay.

Frances: He wants you to see how beautiful it is where he is. He's standing before you now, wanting you to see. He also needs your help with something.

(Tom enters, faces Michael.)

Michael: He needs my help?... Tommy.

Tom: Hi Mike.

Michael: You don't look the same. You sound the same, though. Are you glowing?

Tom: You're seeing a dimension of light. It's fantastic here, Mike. All these angels. There really are angels. And they're beautiful. Me too. I'm one of them.

Michael: I miss you.

Tom: I know. I'm hangin' around all the time. You don't pay very close attention.

Michael: What do you mean, hangin' around. Angels don't talk like that. Angels don't say hangin'.

Tom: Who says?

Michael:	Okay. What do I know? What do you mean, you know? You know what I'm feeling? How?
Tom:	I've been near you a lot. I've seen what you've been through.
Michael:	Yeah?
Tom:	Yeah.
Michael:	Everything? Even Marilyn? You know what I went through with Marilyn?
Tom:	It's not like that. It's not every little detail.
Michael:	Oh, that's good. I was kinda a dick with Marilyn. I hope you weren't watchin'. Listen, I gotta tell you somethin'. I'm sorry about a lot of things I did to you when we were kids. I never got a chance to make it up to you.
Tom:	Forget it. No big deal.
Michael:	No, it is a big deal. I've been waiting a long time to say this. I feel bad about ditchin' you all the time and tellin' you stories to scare you. I shoulda' said this when you were alive.
Tom:	I know. Mike, forget those things. They don't matter.
Michael:	Don't tell me they don't matter, they do matter. I've felt bad for a lot of years and I want to tell you this, so shut up and listen. I'm sorry, I didn't mean that. It's just that after you died, I realized you're the only person who looked up to me. Even after I did all those shit things to you. I realized I had only one little brother who was going to look up to me and that was you and I wished I'd understood that while you were alive. Everything was so fucked up in our house. Is that okay that I said fuck in front of you? Are angels okay with that shit?
Tom:	Yes, it's fine. But that's what I wanted to talk to you about. There are problems. It would be better to face them.
Michael:	I'm not exactly the heroic type.
Tom:	Do you know what I'm talking about?
Michael:	Yes, no, maybe – what are you talking about?
Tom:	Mom's an alcoholic and so full of rage.
Michael:	Yeah, duh.
Tom:	She's going to push Sue right over the edge. Only Suzie'll never survive, she's not as tough as Mom.
Michael:	What?
Tom:	Mom will never allow Suzie to be a success. She's competing with her. Sue keeps trying. Can't you see how frantic she's becoming? No matter what she does Mom undermines her confidence. She's very clever – but it's obvious once you know what she's doing.
Michael:	So, what is it I'm supposed to do?

Tom:	Sue wants to move away.
Michael:	She does?
Tom:	You actually know this.
Michael:	I do?
Tom:	You do. Think.
Michael:	You mean the thing with her friends in San Francisco?
Tom:	Yes.
Michael:	That's a serious thing?
Tom:	Yes. She's too afraid to talk about it. You have to encourage her. Tell her to go. Tell her you believe in her.
Michael:	I didn't come here to plan Suzie's life. I came here because I wanted to know about you.
Tom:	This is about me. You think just 'cause I'm not living here on earth that our life together is over?
Michael:	No – well – I don't know. That's what I'm trying to find out. Now you're hitting me with all this about Suzie.
Tom:	It's all connected. You think you're the only one with regrets? If you ever wanted to do something for me – this is it. Help Suzie. Help her get out of there. Help her have her own life.
Michael:	I don't even have my own life. How the hell am I supposed to help her?
Tom:	You'll see.
Michael:	I will?
Tom:	I didn't mean to die. I haven't finished my life with you guys. I shouldn't have died when I did. It was my own fault, but it was a colossal mistake.
Michael:	You know – none of us have ever had the guts to tell Mom and Dad that you were high when you died.
Tom:	Yeah, I know. It wouldn't kill them to know. Might even shock 'em into sobriety. I'll tell you this; none of you is as breakable as you think – except Suzie.
Michael:	Why do you think she's so weak? She's a lot like Mom.
Tom:	She emulates Mom 'cause she wants Mom to love her and respect her...It's not she herself who's weak. It's the hook in her. She's trying to aim at something she's doomed to fail at because Mom can't love her. The situation will break her spirit. If she goes now she'll gain her life back, she'll do all she's capable of doing. If she stays, she'll die inside. Please help her.
Michael:	Of course I will. If I can.

Tom: Of course you can. You'll do better than you think. I've got to go,
                we're draining Frances' batteries. She can't hold this space forever.
                Thanks Mike, I love you. You're a good brother. Please promise
                me you'll forget all those things that you think were so bad. They
                were kid stuff. So promise, okay?

Michael: I promise. Will I ever see you again?

Tom: I hope so. Bye.

Michael: Bye Tom-Tom. Hey, remember we used to call you that?

(Tom has gone.)

                Tom? Tommy? Tom-Tom?

Frances: Don't worry Michael, he's still here with you. You just can't see
                him. It would be too chaotic if we held open the veils between the
                worlds for too long. We have to accept our physical lives and trust
                that the life of spirit is within us and around us always, even if we
                can't see it.

Rolling Stone

Premise: **Scott** I am a man, he is a man; we have a relationship, he is my brother. We are at Mom's house.

Winky I am a man, he is a man; we have a relationship, he is my brother. We are at Mom's house.

Grace I am a woman, they are men; we have a
relationship, they are my sons. We are in my home.

Scott:	Hey Wink, long time.
Winky:	Hey dude. Everything bright and perky in your life?
Scott:	What?
Winky:	Your goal in life. Everything goin' the way you want it?
Scott:	Bright and perky?
Winky:	That's just the image. You know…cool and groovy. Don't get bent, just doin' the relating thing. Respect of your process and all.
Scott:	When did you give up speaking English?
Winky:	English is a big language. Lotta words in it.
Scott:	This is going to be long weekend.
Winky:	Gobble gobble.
Scott:	Christ.
Grace:	Winky! Darling, it's good to see you. I'm so glad you're here. You look wonderful, doesn't he Scott?
Scott:	Fab.
Winky:	Hi Mom.
Grace:	I'm glad you both are here. I want to talk to you before everyone's here.
Winky:	Debriefing?
Scott:	What is it, Mom?

Grace:	You know Poppy's coming and she's bringing her friend, Jade.
Winky:	Severe. Jade, sounds…something, severe. Exotic.
Grace:	Wink…Anyway, your father and I have talked it all over and we want to make her feel just as welcome as...well, you know.
Winky:	As a heterosexual?
Scott:	Control your attitude, for just, what? An hour could you?
Grace:	Oh boys, please don't fight. I can't bear it if you do. It's Thanksgiving.
Scott:	We know it's Thanksgiving Mom.
Winky:	Ooh, is that a little attitude I detect.
Scott:	Fuck you.
Grace:	Scotty, please.
Scott:	Well what are you trying to tell us? To be nice to Poppy's girlfriend? What do you think we'd do? You think you and Dad are the only one's who know how to be polite?
Grace:	I don't know. I really don't know. I'm just nervous. Poppy must be nervous and I want her to feel at home like the rest of us.
Winky:	Don't worry Mom, I have lots of lesbian friends. I'll know how to act.
Grace:	I hope you're not making fun of me.
Winky:	Just a little. Relax. If you're this tense when Poppy gets here she's gonna know it. Then she'll start in with her weird shit, Dad'll start probing and all hell will break loose.
Grace:	Either of you got a Valium?
Winky:	Gave 'em up when I was sixteen. Don't worry, we'll be good little soldiers.
Grace:	I know you will, and Winky…take a little time with your father, just you two. He's missed you.
Winky:	Sure. Scott'll brush me up on the father and son lingo. I'm a little rusty.
Scott:	Just speak English and don't be condescending. You ought to do fine.
Winky:	I'm not condescending, just uncomfortable.
Grace:	Just act like you're glad to see him, okay?
Winky:	For Christ's sake, Mom, why do you think I came home? You're my family, he's my father. Why do you say things like that? "Just pretend I'm happy to see him". He's my father.
Scott:	Lay off her, Warren.
Winky:	Warren? You sound like Dad when you call me Warren. Mom, just stop trying to control things. You treat us like we haven't

got any brains. "Be nice to Poppy and Jade". She's my sister…
"Pretend with your father", it's bullshit. Just let us have our own
relationships with each other, please. It's insulting.

Grace: Everyone's so damn testy, it makes me nervous.

Winky: We wouldn't be testy if you didn't treat us like dunces.

Scott: We'll be okay, Mom. Honest.

Grace: I know. I know. Really, I do know that. I'm just a little neurotic.
I don't even know when it happened. There wasn't one day I
woke up and felt different. I know I was normal once. I thought
motherhood was going to be great. And it is, don't get me wrong,
it's just so stressful. My home-ec teacher never discussed how to
be good to lesbians or how to manage alienated brothers. How'd
we all get this way? A bunch of strangers is what we are. I still
look at you and see you as the children I knew. Then you say
something odd or abrupt and I have to look at you as adults and
I realize you really are strangers to me. My own children. It's a
shock. I just have to get use to it, that's all.

Winky: I came home because I miss you all. I love you. I hope you can
believe that.

Scott: I love you Mom. I even love Warren. You know that don't you?

Grace: Well, I love you all more than anything. You two, Poppy,
Abby, you're my life, you and your father. Let's have a happy
Thanksgiving, okay?

Scott & Winky: Okay.

Sir

Premise: **Dawn** I am a woman, he is a man; we have a relationship, he is my boyfriend. We are at a restaurant. It's my first day in Los Angeles.

Nick I am a man, she is a woman; we have a relationship, she is my girlfriend. We are in a restaurant. Tonight I'm going to "pop the question".

Chauncey I am a man, he is a man; we have a relationship, he is a regular customer. We are in the restaurant where I work. I haven't met his girlfriend. The allergy medicine didn't work right.

Dawn: Nicky, this is beautiful. I'm impressed.

Nick: Well don't be. And don't call me Nicky. I'm Nick now.

Dawn: Then Nick it is.

Nick: Now stop gawkin' and be cool. The thing is in places like this you gotta remain unimpressed. They won't let you in if they see your eyes buggin' out like a tourist.

Dawn: Nicky. Nick. Sorry. Will you relax, please. I'm not going to have any fun if you keep telling me what to do.

Nick: I'm sorry, Dawn. It's just the way things are here. Look around you. What do you see? Not one of them looks impressed. They've all got this attitude of entitlement. See what I mean?

Dawn: I'm sure they're still enjoying themselves. Let's order. I'm starving.

Nick: How 'bout some oysters and a white Bordeaux?

(Chauncey enters)

Dawn: Perfect.

Chauncey: Good evening Mr. Bromin. What will it be to start?

Nick: Are the oysters good tonight, Chauncey?

Chauncey:	Excellent sir.
Nick:	Good, and we'll have whatever your best year is in a white Bordeaux.
Chauncey:	Very well sir, I have an oxlent Margeaux. Excuse me, I mean excellent. A Chateau Margeaux. I think you'll be plizzed – pleased. If you'll excuse me.

(Chauncey exits)

Dawn:	He seems a little distracted.
Nick:	Yeah.
Dawn:	So he knows you by name. Mr. Bromin, sir.
Nick:	It's part of the act. Everyone has everyone else fooled. The people who come here to eat think the waiters won't wait on you unless you're someone special. And the waiters are all hoping they'll get cast in the role of a lifetime standing there with the grilled tuna in tomatillo sauce.
Dawn:	That's pitiful.
Nick:	Yeah, well. They've been doing it so long they all think they're something special.
Dawn:	Including you?
Nick:	They all got to take their pants down to shit.
Dawn:	Nicky.
Nick:	Nick.
Dawn:	What's the matter with you?
Nick:	None of these turds are special.

(Chauncey enters)

Dawn:	This is becoming offensive, Nicky.
Nick:	Nick.
Chauncey:	Your wine, sir. Margeaux '76.
Nick:	Is this real dust or do you spray it on the bottle before you serve it?
Chauncey:	Even Hollywood has its limits Mr. Bromin. The dust is real, no bout adoubt it. No doubt about it. Will you be tasting the wine or will the lady?
Nick:	I will. Everything okay Chaunce?
Chauncey:	Fine sir. *(Pours the wine.)* There sir. See if that suits your taste Mr. Bromin, sir.
Nick:	You're good Chauncey, never let me down.
Chauncey:	Thank you sir. May I suggest the rack of lamb tonight?
Nick:	That will be fine. Now how about those oysters first?
Chauncey:	Sirlly, surely. I have wings on my feet.

(Chauncey exits)

Nick: He's acting weird tonight.

Dawn: Aren't you uncomfortable with him calling you "sir" all the time?

Nick: I treat him good, he shows me respect.

Dawn: Treat him good? Like a pet, or a servant?

Nick: I treat him better than the rest of these sleazeballs. See that guy at the corner table? The one who keeps patting his head?

Dawn: Yes.

Nick: Saul Bosnick. If he ever lets you close enough to him, you could see how his hair is planted in rows. He keeps patting it to be sure it's still there.

(Chauncey enters)

Dawn: Why don't you like these men, Nick?

Nick: Hell, they wouldn't know what to do if anyone liked them. Would they, Chauncey?

Chauncey: "Lez oysters", Monsieur. Cold, fresh and slimy. Tasty, I mean tasty.

Nick: Chauncey, that's not very funny.

Chauncey: I'm sorry sir, it wasn't meant to be funny.

Nick: I mean a comment like that could offend the lady.

Chauncey: It wasn't meant to offend, sure, I assir you. In fact, it wasn't meant for anything, it just slipped out. I'm terribly sorry.

Dawn: Really Chauncey, it's okay…It was actually funny. If someone had a sense of humor he'd be laughing I'm sure.

Nick: Get a grip there Chauncey, this is a special evening. I don't want anything to spoil it.

Chauncey: I'm needed in the kitchen, sir. If there's nothing else.

Nick: No, we're fine. Thanks.

(Chauncey exits)

           I don't get it. He's usually smooth as silk.

Dawn: Anyone can have a bad day.

Nick: Well, he can have it on his own time, not while I'm payin' the tab.

Dawn: Nick Martin, what on earth is the matter with you. You're acting like a gold plated bore.

Nick: Do you know what this dinner is costing me?

Dawn: I don't care what it costs, but it's going to cost you something a lot more dear, if you don't get that wild hair out of your ass.

Nick: Dawn, I'm shocked.

Dawn:	Is that the only way to get through to you? To be vulgar and harsh? What's happened to you Nick? Why are you so full of judgment? My god, you've got a great new job, a chance to meet and work with some of the top people in the business. You talk about them like they're vile to you. Haven't you made friends with any of them?
Nick:	Not in Hollywood. They don't want you to be friends, they want you to be afraid of them.
Dawn:	That's too bad. Then I feel sorry for them.
Nick:	Don't waste your sympathy. This is no place for your spiritual malarkey. This is the real world.
Dawn:	You're not going to do it to me, Nick. Take me back to the hotel.
Nick:	What?
Dawn:	You're not going to tear me down with all the others.
Nick:	I'm not tearin' you down. It's just the way it is out here. The sooner you know that, the better off you'll be.
Dawn:	That's ridiculous. How you feel towards other human beings doesn't change from place to place. My God, there is a whole universe which is somehow held together. You think L.A. is somehow disengaged from the whole?
Nick:	No, it is the hole. The asshole of the universe.

(she stands)

Dawn:	That does it, Nick. I'll get a cab.
Nick:	Hey, sit down. I didn't mean anything.
Dawn:	I will not sit down. You've changed, Nick. You're cruel and twisted and vulgar. It's not this city. It's you.

(Chauncey enters)

Chauncey:	The rack of…You're not leaving? Jeez, we got it out as fast as possible. It's cooked to perfection. I mean as good as that flabby ass slob of a cook can get it. Oh, what did I say?
Nick:	Please sit down. I'm sorry.
Chauncey:	No, I can't. We're not allowed to sit with the customers in this fascist place.
Nick:	Not you. Dawn.
Chauncey:	I didn't mean that. Actually, I did mean it but I didn't mean to say it…out loud.
Nick:	What the hell's the matter with you?
Chauncey:	Not quite sure sir. Is that right? Sure sir, sir sure, sure sure, that's easy for you to say.
Dawn:	I'm going.

Nick:	No! Please, I'm sorry. Chauncey: No! Please, I'll get fired.
Nick:	This isn't about you, Chauncey.
Chauncey:	Then what's the problem?
Nick:	What's your problem?
Chauncey:	I don't have a problem, bub. What's your problem? I'm sorry. I didn't mean that. I don't know what's the matter with me.
Dawn:	Sit down Chauncey, you look a little pale. Are you drunk?
Chauncey:	God no, I don't drink.
Nick:	Dawn, can't that wait?
Dawn:	Something's wrong with him, Nick. Chauncey, I'm a nurse. Have you taken any medication today?
Chauncey:	Yeah.
Dawn:	What did you take?
Chauncey:	I borrowed some of my roommate's allergy medicine. I ran out of mine.
Dawn:	What kind? Prescription? Do you have any more with you?
Chauncey:	Yeah, here.
Dawn:	You got these from your roommate? What does he do?
Chauncey:	He's a veterinarian's technician. He works for veterinarians in animal acts and circuses, things like that. That's hard to say.
Dawn:	You didn't take the allergy medicine, Chauncey. You've taken an animal sedative, a powerful one. Probably used on the big cats, or bears or something like that. We better get you to an emergency room. Go get the car, Nick.
Nick:	This isn't our problem, Dawn.
Dawn:	Just do it, Nick.
Nick:	His boss can call someone – I've got a big…
Dawn:	Think about someone else for a change.
Nick:	I am.
Dawn:	The car, Nick. Now!
Nick:	Okay, okay…I really love you, you know. It's just this town got to me. I'm gonna be okay, I promise.
Dawn:	We'll talk about it later, Nick. He's gonna pass out.
Nick:	I'm going. I really love you. I want you to marry me. That's why the dinner and your trip out here…I can't take this place on my own. I need you, Dawn. Will you marry me?
Dawn:	Forget the car, call 911.
Nick:	Will you marry me?
Dawn:	He's going fast.

(Nick dials on his cell phone.)

Nick: Will you marry me?

Chauncey: Say "yes" Dawn, please.

Dawn: Yes! Alright, yes.

Nick: Did you hear that Chaunce, she said yes. She's gonna marry me.

             (Into phone) Huh? Oh yeah. We got a problem here at Chez Jeff.

Dawn: It's an O.D., tell 'em it's an O.D.

Nick:	Dawn:
An O.D.	*(Slapping him gently)*
Tranquilizers.	Chauncey, stay awake!
Very fast, please.	Stay with me.
They are on their way.	

Chauncey: Night-night.

Dawn: It's important you stay
             awake, Chauncey. Talk
             to me.

Chauncey: Hmphpfft.

Nick: Hang in there champ. Help is on the way.

             (To Dawn) I love you.

(Chauncey's eyes focus on Nick – confused.)

Nick: *(To Chauncey)* Not you. Dawn.

Washing Dishes

Premise: **Jean** I am a woman, they are women; we have a relationship, we are sisters. We are in Mom's kitchen.

Ann I am a woman, they are women; we have a relationship, we are sisters. We are in Mom's kitchen.

Claire I am a woman, they are women; we have a relationship, we are sisters. We are in Mom's kitchen.

Jean: I think you should apologize to Mom. There was no reason to be so mean to her at dinner in front of her friends.

Ann: Thank you for sharing.

Jean: Don't be such a bitch.

Ann: Mind your own business.

Claire: Jesus, Ann, when are you going to get over it?

Ann: Get over what?

Claire: Whatever sends you off about Mom. She didn't do anything to warrant that.

Ann: Well aren't you two the dutiful little daughters.

Jean: Don't be so goddamned sarcastic. You are not on very solid ground.

Ann: What're you gonna do, beat me up? Aren't we a little old for that?

Claire: If not for that, I would have punched you in the mouth at dinner.

Ann: You make me puke.

Jean: You have no right to ruin everyone's time because you're so unhappy.

Ann: Who says I'm unhappy?

Jean:	Who needs to?
Ann:	Fuck you.
Claire:	Are you going to do this the rest of your life? Just be mean and strike out when things don't go your way?
Ann:	Why don't you ask Mom that?
Claire:	Mom didn't strike out.
Ann:	She doesn't have to. She's covert and manipulative. She's fucking nuts and you two act like she's the fucking Queen Mum.
Jean:	You're not the only one who grew up with her. We did too. We know how she's been, but she's let go of a lot. She's doing the best she can.
Ann:	Well so am I. Why don't you give me the same benefit of the doubt?
Jean:	We do constantly. I get an acid stomach whenever you're around. I'm just waiting for the...fucking time bomb to go off when you two are together.
Ann:	I'll give you some Maalox.
Ann:	You think that's my fault?
Claire:	Yes. You've always done it.
Ann:	That's not fair. I didn't make Mom a raging beast.
Claire:	You're right. You didn't. But you also didn't have her life.
Ann:	No. I had mine and that was bad enough.
Jean:	We all had the same life. She went off on all of us. She had four kids to raise. She had a lot of pressure and...
Ann:	Don't give me the sob story.
Jean:	Well, since I've had my own children, I understand her frustration better. I only have two and a husband. I don't know how she did it with four on her own. Every parent reaches a breaking point, I have. Maybe that's why I can forgive her. If you'd had children, you might have.
Ann:	You bitch, how dare you throw that in my face?!

Jean: I wasn't throwing it in your
face, I just meant that you
would know what it's like.   Jean: Please, Ann, I'm sorry. I...

                                   Ann: What? That would make

Claire: Hold it you guys, ease up.   me whole?

                                   Claire: That's not what she meant.

Ann:	Why should I have children in a fucked up world like this? You think you're better because you have children. What gift is life when it's based on such bullshit.

Jean:	You missed my point completely.
Ann:	And you've missed mine completely.
Claire:	For God's sake, Ann, grow up. This isn't a competition.
Ann:	Then what is it? When you two decide I'm unacceptable? What am I supposed to do? I don't have any choice, but to fight back.
Claire:	But you start the fights.
Ann:	I do not.
Jean:	You do. You're passive aggressive. You disappear right when Mom serves dinner, because you know it hurts her. You came for dinner for Christ's sake. Where do you go when you disappear?
Ann:	She can't eat without me? She needs me to cut her food, or chew it for her?
Claire:	This is so god damned typical. Why do you suppose we come here?
Ann;	Because you're afraid to say no.
Jean:	Speak for yourself.
Ann:	I come for a free meal.
Claire:	Then don't come. I'll send you a check.
Jean:	Ann, we have a right to have a relationship with Mom. And you do not have the right to spoil our time together.
Ann:	You spoil it yourself.
Claire and Jean:	No, you do.
Ann:	This is classic. Don't you realize this is what Mom has done to us all our lives. She sets two against one. She's the bad seed in this family. She invites you two so you'll protect her.
Jean:	Get some therapy, Ann. You have no excuse not to have healed this stuff. There are twelve step programs if you don't have money for a therapist. There are also clinics with sliding scale, so you really have no excuse except that you have this destructive need to hurt Mom. I won't put up with it.
Ann:	Bully for you.
Jean:	This is it. I won't see you again after this unless you get some help. Not until you have been in a program or therapy for at least six months.
Ann:	Fine, have it your way. Get lost. Why wait, just go now.
Jean:	I'm not leaving here 'till you're gone. I don't trust you with Mom.
Ann:	Aren't you a good little piglet, sucking on the big pig's tit. I hate to break it to you, her tits went dry a long time ago. You're not gonna get what you want.

(Jean slaps Ann.)

Jean: Shut up! I will not listen to you one minute longer.

Claire: Christ, I can't stand this. Look, Ann, I know you feel backed into
             a corner right now. But you bring it on yourself. If Mom and Jean
             and I want to spend quality time together, we have a right to. If
             you can't be with us in the same spirit, then we'll arrange it on our
             own, but we will have it and you won't wreck it. Do you get that?

Ann: Of course I get it. Same old shit.

Claire: I'm sorry you feel that way, but it doesn't change the way I feel.

Ann: Fine.

(Ann leaves.)

Claire: You alright?

Jean: Felt damn good to hit her.

Claire: I'm more than a little jealous.

Jean: But I feel immensely sad too.

Claire: This was inevitable.

Jean: Yes.

Claire: That was scary.

Jean: No one's ever really told her how wrong she is.

Claire: The irony is that Mom was a tyrant when we were growing up.
             And now Ann is; she's become what she hated the most.

Jean: Tell me tomorrow's another day.

Claire: Tomorrow *is* another day.

Jean: It's what Mom always says. Makes me feel better. Stupid, huh?
             The next day was never much different than the day before.

Claire: I think it's cumulative. These days things are better than when we
             were kids.

Jean: I don't feel very grown up at the moment. Actually, that's not true.
             I feel kinda' primal. Like a panther protecting her clan. Tooth and
             nail sort of thing.

Claire: Well Xena, we better check on Mom. Be sure Ann hasn't sawed
             off one of the legs of her chair.

Jean: Don't.

Claire: What?

Jean: Make me have to kill her.

Claire: I wouldn't put it past her.

Jean: Don't start.

Working Late

Premise: **Rick** I am a man, he is a man; we have a relationship, we work together. We are in our office. It is late at night.

Bill I am a man, he is a man; we have a relationship, we work together. We are in our office. It is late at night.

Entity I am that I am. They are men. William has opened a channel through which we can communicate.

Rick: These your notes? "There is no thought in consciousness." "Feeling and consciousness are one." What does it mean?

Bill: It means God and your balls are the same.

Rick: You're loco.

Bill: Maybe.

Rick: Completely.

Bill: Give me my notebook.

Rick: What else you got in here?

Bill: Nothing that would matter to you.

Rick: Really?

Bill: Gimme the notebook, Dick.

Rick: Rick, my name is Rick.

Bill: Dick.

Rick: Touch-ee...What's this? "Matter is organized intelligence". Where do you come up with this.

Bill: *(Grabs notebook away from Rick.)* I just like to think outside the box.

Rick: I think you're outside the whole store.

Bill:	How can you be in this field and not wonder about the origins of thought and the function of consciousness?
Rick:	I connect the wires, I test the programs. I mean, what does that stuff mean?
Bill:	Perhaps nothing—it just is.
Rick:	So why think about it?
Bill:	You're right, let's get back to work. What's on your monitor?
Rick:	Hmmm. Which disc do you have in?
Bill:	F-ninety-DL.
Rick:	That's funny.
Bill:	What's funny.
Rick:	I'm getting an entrance request code on channel three.
Bill:	Impossible. That's a blank channel on this disc.
Rick:	I know, but I'm getting a very clear request.
Bill:	There's no way one of our users could access that channel with this disc in.
Rick:	Well, Billy-boy, you got a big kink in your program.
Bill:	Well let's see what happens if we give access.
Rick:	What the fuck? Look at my screen. It's chaos.
Bill:	Hmmm. That's interesting.
Rick:	It's scrambling – faster and faster.
Entity:	Hello William Weston.
Rick:	Did you program it to talk to you?
Bill:	No.
Rick:	It knows your name. What have you been doing with this computer? Who are you tied into?
Bill:	Nobody, nothing. I swear. I was just fooling around last night with some theories of physics. I was applying some sound amplification principles to hypothetical spectrum wavelengths to see if there was a way to alter color wavelengths and create new ones. By accelerating them.
Rick:	I think that was too much for this system. This sucker is glowing like, like I don't know what.
Bill:	Rick, it talked to me.
Rick:	Yeah.
Entity:	Actually "It" is not speaking to you. "It" is a machine. Now there is no more need for mechanical assistance. You have created a direct vibrational channel through which we may communicate. Very clever, William. We normally rely on other human entities not unlike yourself.

Bill:	Who are you?
Rick:	Who cares who it is. Shut that thing off.
Bill:	No way.
Entity:	Rick, you need not be fearful.
Rick:	It knows my name. What's going on? Bill – are you a spy?
Bill:	Do I look like a spy?
Rick:	What do I know?
Bill:	Who are you?
Entity:	I am a soul just like you.
Rick:	Right.
Entity:	I no longer live in a human body.
Rick:	You an extraterrestrial?
Entity:	I'm not one of the ones that visit earth in the manner you imagine, no…but I am similar.
Rick:	Jesus! Holy mother of God!
Entity:	Very expressive.
Bill:	*(To Rick)* Maintain, huh?
Rick:	Maintain what? What exactly do I have to hold on to?
Entity:	We must not waste time.
Bill:	Shut up – it's talking.
Entity:	We will be interrupted shortly. One of your armed forces tracking stations is intercepting our frequency.
Bill:	Why are you here? What do you want?
Entity:	To demonstrate that you're on the right track. Keep following your instincts. We will be able to communicate while the frequency band is activated. You must develop a shield though – we must withdraw.
Rick:	Bye.
Bill:	No wait. Why is this important?
Rick:	Bye-bye.
Entity:	Human mediums are safer because human frequencies don't attract attention, but human beliefs tend to block certain levels of understanding and human thought forms often misinterpret the communication. The problem with mechanics is they require very noticeable frequencies. Governments and militaries tend to be suspicious.
Bill:	How do I create a shield. Please?
Entity:	We must withdraw now – too much attention now.
Bill:	The shield…What about the…

Entity:	Music. Amplify sub-audial tones. Goodbye.
Bill:	No wait! Wait…Shit! We did it Rick, we did it! Holy Mother of God, we did it! Can you believe it?
Rick:	What'd we do?
Bill:	We pierced the mystic membrane. We accessed the astral plane. We went into the ether.
Rick:	I think you went into something else.
Bill:	It's amazing. Pure consciousness. Pure intelligence. It's a frequency.
Rick:	Yeah.
Bill:	We're gonna be famous!
Rick:	What do you mean "we"? You try to explain this to Mort in the morning. We no longer have a secure program. Little E.T.s are getting in, you see… Yeah, Mort will understand. Pink slips for Bill and Rick. No one would hire us after that.
Bill:	Rick, Rickmeister – you just don't get it.
Rick:	No Bill. Billy-willy, you don't get it. Listen to what you're saying. Famous? You tell anyone about this and you're gonna be locked up. You'll disappear.
Bill:	But there's a value in this – this answers so many questions.
Rick:	The only questions you'll be answering are the military tribunal's. In an unknown location with indescribable torture techniques.
Bill:	That can't be so.
Rick:	Read the Patriot Act.
Bill:	But this is a scientific breakthrough.
Rick:	This is a fuckin' nightmare.
Bill:	I gotta work on the shield.
Rick:	Listen. You won't take it personally if I disavow you? I wasn't here tonight, okay? I never met you.
Bill:	That's very touching, thank you. What's your favorite rock song?
Rick:	Sympathy for the Devil.

Female
Monologues

Breaking Free

Premise: I am a woman, my name is Sue; I am with Michael's
best friend Jeff. We are in my apartment. Michael hit
me and knocked me down. In the aftermath, Jeff just
told me he loves me.

Now you've said it. Now we can't pretend anymore. Now
you've busted the whole thing wide open and I have to do something
because I can't face Michael now. Now I can't ever be in the same
damn room with him because he'll know. He'll know it's you and me
against him. His worst fears will be confirmed and he will kill me. In
fact, why don't you just kill me now and get it over with. Go ahead.
Just strangle me or stab me or something. Do it, Jeff. Quick! Before he
comes back. Be quick and merciful. Because he won't. He'll torture
me. Long drawn out torture. The kind he's best at. God damn it, why
did you have to tell me this now? I don't know what is real anymore.
I thought I knew why you're always around. Or at least I hoped I did,
but I'm so scared. Sometimes I'm sure I'm kidding myself; a way
to have hope where there is no hope. I've been thinking I'm losing
my mind Jeff. I was too afraid to think you really love me. I'm so
ashamed that my life got to be this way. My feelings are very fucked
up. I have this unreasonable fear, like something horrible is about to
happen. I want to scream and run for the hills and at the same time
laugh and fall down and hug you and kiss you…but this is probably
some syndrome, that prisoners get when they're about to be executed,
I think. Like Ann Boleyn right before King Henry had her beheaded.
I'm nuts, I'm sorry. What, what, what are we supposed to do now?
I'm babbling. But I really feel like I gotta get out of here. He's gonna
come back. To make sure I'm not talking to anybody.

Dear Henry

Premise: I am a woman, my name is Melissa. I am writing a
letter to Henry. I am in my bedroom.

Henry dear, I want to be as clear as possible. If my words seem
too carefully chosen, it's because they are. Please forgive the absent
sense of newness in this. I find myself to be intimate with only two
aspects of your personality. I have faith that you, like other people,
have your more subtle facets.

Regarding your sense of contentment and your relationships,
I think you would be well served if you could keep in mind that
that which you perceive as the right way to perform a task, convey
a thought, or, say, to create a sense of well-being, is merely your
way. Not *the* way. And your way, my darling, is, at its broadest, one-
dimensional. Maybe it's not that you have such strong prejudice, but
that your expression of self is so lacking in compassion, insight and
intelligence.

I have compassion for you. To the extent that you are a member
of the human race and born with the same unknowingness as the
rest of us. But your congenital inability to recognize within yourself
the possibility of error cuts short my sense of caring. Nips it in the
goddamn bud.

Did you know my heart ached for you when your tragic
error was uncovered? Yes, the television reporter was dogged in
his determination to find out the facts. Watching the television
interrogation was agonizing for me. I saw in you a child who could
not grasp what had happened to him. I saw that to have erred was,
for you, the greatest of tragedies. I saw then how the need to be right
forms all your thoughts, all your actions. I finally understood why you
look upon me and my feelings as a child regards a waterfall: wide-
eyed, but from a safe distance.

You tell me I should not feel negativity when my humanity is
denied. You say that resentment and anger have no place in the new
age. You are not the universal soldier, Henry. What you are, Henry,

is a turd. A cosmic turd. Your appreciation for the Hopi Indians and their ritual fire dance is deep, but that alone does not give you rank among the great prophets of our time. You say the wind blows through you because you give it no resistance. I think the wind can only blow through a space that is empty.

It is my belief, Henry, and I allow that I could be wrong, that evolution and higher consciousness are found in the understanding which emerges with the expression of our feelings. But one must have feelings in order for that to occur. I wish I could see this as a great cosmic joke and laugh as I bid you farewell. It is beyond your ability to conceive that you might make an oversight that isn't divinely guided or that you might have a simple lapse of memory. That sort of arrogance, handsome one, is more dangerous than words can say.

My earlier impulses ran toward annihilation, but I really do understand, when a person has no self worth, all that's left to him is arrogance. What you do is who you are, Henry. What you think means nothing. I know what you're thinking now, but I assure you, this missive is not born of envy. I am most happy to have been born a woman. This woman. And shall henceforth live my life in my own way, as is my right. Bidding you the fondest farewell.

Love, Melissa

Filling The Gap

Premise: I am a woman, my name is Peggy. I am speaking to
my daughter. We are in my home.

You know during the war every day was filled with death. And a poignant sense of purpose in being alive. Whether you chose it or not, you were part of the war effort. We watched our boys get on buses and trains and ships knowing most of them weren't coming back. But we pretended otherwise. Whenever there were more than two of us we made a party. We sought each other out. We made ourselves busy at work and then we gathered together at night. Whoever was available. And we drank god-awful amounts of hooch. We didn't give ourselves time to think.

We gave up so many things so the soldiers would have the supplies they needed to win the war. We couldn't see beyond the moment when the war would end for us, and our own suffering would be relieved. So we cheered when Hiroshima and Nagasaki were destroyed. Good had triumphed over evil. We were the good guys. Emperor Hirohito was still alive of course and surrendered to the Allies. But in those two cities, the old, the young, everyone suffered in ways we hadn't imagined was possible. The lucky ones died. The collective wisdom of the world could not find a humane way to end that war. The greatest generation. We opened the door to a world of inconceivable horror. I fear sometimes that mankind won't recover.

I try not to think that. It seems unpatriotic. It would mean that all the boys and men who died for the right reasons had ultimately failed or been betrayed by a worse enemy within our own psyches. They fought to make a better world. We killed and maimed thousands of innocent people in order to scare their leaders into submission. There is no wisdom in that and there is certainly nothing moral about it. At the time we saw it as the only solution.

I feel responsible for being so short-sighted. Me and everyone else who felt only the relief of our war ending. Our boys were coming home. We cheered and cried for days after we got the news. If we worried, we didn't show it. Now we all know what those bombs did and how the suffering they caused hasn't ended. And the potential for worse destruction has grown ever since. Every generation finds something to hold it together. If it's not something good, it'll be something bad perhaps.

First Edition

Premise: I am a woman, my name is Cecile. I am on my way to the doctor's office. My first non-fiction book is about to be released.

This is a great moment in my life, it should feel good. Why do I feel so vile?

God, it's hot. Am I having a heart attack? No. One doesn't feel hot during a heart attack. How do I know that? I don't know what a heart attack feels like.

My feet are numb. Maybe it's menopause. You get hot with menopause. Do your feet get numb? Mother's feet never went numb. It's a heart attack. Shit, my first non-fiction is about to go on the shelves and I'm going to die of a heart attack before the first copy sells.

I hope Dr. Fisk doesn't keep me waiting. I think I'll embarrass myself if I have to wait. Everyone will stare at me. They'll know something is wrong. That woman is having a breakdown. Christ! Is that what this is? Am I having a breakdown? I should have had more books under my belt before a breakdown. Second attempt, okay, but coolly received; third attempt was a personal triumph, but critically controversial. That's when the breakdown comes. Not as the first one hits the stands.

I should never have done this. I should have known. There's instability in the family. Now the whole world will know. If the book flops, no one will care. If the book is a success then this is going to be very embarrassing. To be receiving residuals at the residential treatment center.

Fuck you Dad. I wish you hadn't killed yourself. I wish you hadn't embezzled. I wish I'd never said yes to Helen.

Why is this happening to me? Why are my feet numb? I could get a cab. I can't. I don't think I can talk. I think I better keep walking.

Alright Cecile, get a grip. It's just a book. This isn't about the book. The book is great. I'm excited. Why do I feel like I'm dying? I am dying. That's why I feel like I'm dying. My God, I'm not imagining this. I'm dying. Jesus! Where am I? I've gone past it. I've passed the god-damned doctor's office. No. No. I don't think I've passed it yet. Nothing looks familiar. No, there's the Kroger's. The Kroger's comes before the bank and the bank comes before the medical building... Or is that from the other direction? God help me, I'm lost and I'm dying right here on a busy street in the middle of the god-damned day. Bright sunlight. Stark raving sunlight. Stark raving...raving...raving lunatic.

Come on, Cecile, come on! You're not dead yet. My feet are still numb. My heart is speeding up. It's hot. What's that smell? It's death. It's the grim reaper... he's here and he smells bad. Dear God, I'm not ready to go. I want to see how my book does. I want to see Jonathan graduate from high school. College. I want to see him married. I want to know his children.

Cecile, lighten up. My mind is moving on its own. I can't control it. This is how it happens. It lives in you like a virus. Then, when you ask too much of life – when you push yourself too hard for something more you trigger it and zappo! You're cuckoo. That must be what happened to Dad. And now it's happening to me because the virus is in me.

Damn you, Dad. You fucker. Damn you for infecting me with your virus. Damn you for being weak and giving up and leaving us here to figure out who the fuck you really were. I've done something Dad, something I'm proud of. I want to enjoy it. I don't want to die. I don't want to crumble into a quivering, gibbering mass of raw nerve endings which is what I'm beginning to feel like here. Right fucking here and now.

Dear Jesus, there's the building. My heart is going to give out before I get there. Dear Lord, give me strength. Just get me to Dr. Fisk's office, then take me if you must, but not out here in the parking lot. Legs all splayed, face blue, eyes wide and staring. Please, not like that. People will come. They'll know. They'll see by looking at me that I've died of madness. Before one book has sold.

Just like Dad. Just like every other hapless schlump who tried to be an artist. Artists are mad. My god. It wasn't just superstition; I was right. I tapped into my artistic self and I've tapped into my madness. Why didn't I leave it alone? Let it fade away.

I'm making it by God! I'm making it... On numb feet no less. My face is tight. I'm going to cry. Why? I don't want Dr. Fisk to see me this way. Cecile, for Christ sake, he's a doctor. I can't explain it. I'm talking to myself. What's happening to me? Crimony, I'll walk through that door, my face twitching. Everyone will know. They'll see it all over me.

It's cool in here. The air-conditioning feels good. I'm here! I'm shaking. Breathe deep. The doorknob is cold. My hand is slimy. Slimy and shaking. The doorknob is slimy, I can't turn it. Maybe if I just fall against the door it'll open. Or someone will hear and they'll open it. Open up please. Open says-a-me. I'm here. Dr. Fisk. Someone. Someone please open the mother-lovin' door.

Male
Monologues

A Fine Line

Premise: I am a man, My name is Jack. I am speaking to my lover. I am a musician, she is an artist. We are in our apartment.

Loving you isn't enough. I don't feel like I know you anymore. And I wonder if I was more in love with our struggle as artists, your nobility. I don't know why I feel so different now. I love you. I do. Before this, on my bad days I could look at you and think, "she's staying with it. If she can tough it out, so can I." Now on my bad days you're not there struggling beside me, and I feel alone. One little doubt creeps in and I start to unravel inside – you start to look like the enemy to me. Like you've forgotten the struggle already, and if the struggle is so easy to forget, why am I so invested in it? I'm doubting myself. I go so deep down into this emptiness that I look like a stranger to myself. It terrifies me. I want to feel together again. Like we're both living in the same life. Together.

Breaking Free

Premise:　I am a man, my name is Jeff. I am with Michael's wife. We are in her apartment. Michael just hit her and knocked her down.

I can't do this anymore. I can't not tell you how I feel. I can't pretend like I don't know how you feel. This is fuckin' nuts and I don't know what to do exactly, except I know I can't keep doing what I've been doing, which is worse than nothing. I love you, Sue, and I am not going to keep quiet out of respect for your marriage to my fucking best friend who is a god-damned psycho woman hater, because your marriage to that fucker is a dismal tragedy. I know this is not a complete surprise to you. Please, God. Tell me this does not come as a complete surprise to you. It's not getting better, Sue. Isn't that what we were hoping for? That it would get better. It's getting worse. You just said it yourself. He's capable of killing you and the only reason he doesn't is that he enjoys torturing you more. I told you now because you're not safe and he's not my friend. I stopped loving him a year ago. I've been pretending so that I could be around. To make sure he didn't do anything really bad. But we saw it today. Me being here doesn't make any difference anymore. He hit you hard enough to knock you down. I think he knows it hurts you more when someone else is around and sees it. He takes pleasure in that. He's sadistic.

Bury The Dead - 1

Premise: I am a man, my name is Jeff. I am with my brother
            Peter. We are in his home. Dad's funeral was today.

Dad never did anything to anyone or for anyone unless it was to satisfy his own ego. Including jerking you around like a puppet . Get it straight, little brother. You are angry with Dad, not me. But you've put it on me ever since I left here. Grow up, get over it. I don't need to be blamed and hated for living my life the best I know how. We don't ever have to see each other again. Dad's dead, there's no more family. So if that's what you want, just say so. Dad was a stupid mean son of a bitch. He lived life the only way he knew how. You couldn't see what I saw. I don't know why I knew it, but I knew he'd never change. You kept thinking one day he'd give you the respect you deserve. He didn't. And now he's dead. And now you've got to live.

Bury The Dead - 2

Premise: I am a man, my name is Peter. I am with my brother
Jeff. We are in my home. Dad's funeral was today

I've got demons Jeff. I can't stop them. They confuse me. I know it's wrong to feel what I'm feeling. I know there's another better feeling out there. I don't know which way to reach. It all seems like blackness. I don't think I know how. I lived my whole life covering up for Dad. Making excuses for him. Fearing him, wanting him to love me. Hating him for not loving me. Hating you for being free. I'm scared. You want to know how nutty I am? My biggest fear was, that one day he'd just come right out and tell me what he thought of me. That he didn't love me – that he didn't really even like me. That it didn't matter that I was his son. That I was just another person he could manipulate. It seemed like that. The few times he ever looked right at me the look on his face said that. That he just wished I'd go away. I was convinced that he would actually say it one day.

Non-Gender
Specific
Monologues

Where's the Magic?

Premise: I am a teacher, I teach science. I am with my principal.
            We are in his/her office.

I teach science. Science is based on the testing of hypotheses. Nothing, not one god-damned little thing has ever been discovered by accepting that what we know is all there is to know. That's science and that's what I teach. I send them home with questions to discuss. They're not my ideas. If you don't think the hypotheses I present are possible, then tell me what is. After nuclear war, what will happen to the world, to life as we know it? What's the half-life of all the chemical weapons? How do they react to chemicals already in our urban environments? How long do they stay in the ground water? What will they do to sea life as we know it? Can you tell me? Do you know anyone, any-god-damned-one who can tell me so I don't have to worry? Who's going to figure it out? They saw the towers go down. They've seen Armageddon. After nuclear winter, do the trees grow back? Do birds ever fly again? Are there birds? If I'm wrong, you must know what's right. Huh? Fill me in. I'm waiting. After biological warfare, what will future homosapiens look like? I want an answer. Why so quiet? Anthrax got your tongue?

We've got a responsibility here, you and me. Right now. I don't have the answers and I'm sure as hell not going to pretend to these kids that I do. If they don't begin to believe that they have the power to change things, then we might as well just put a gun in our mouths and pull the trigger now.